BUSINESS/SCIENCE/TECHNOLOGY DIVISION
CHICAGO PUBLIC LIBRARY
400 SOUTH STATE STREET
CHICAGO, ILLINOIS 60605

VM
341
.S28
2002

HWLCTC

S0-ABY-598

R0400629890
Chris-Craft of the 1950s

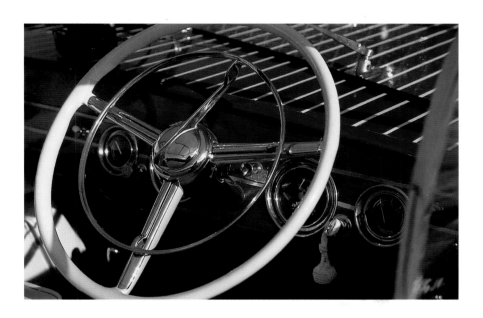

Chris-Craft
of the 1950s

Jack Savage

MBI Publishing Company

Dedicated to the late Joe Gribbins,
who was taken from us too early.

VM
341
.S28
2002

First published in 2002 by MBI Publishing
Company, Galtier Plaza, 380 Jackson Street,
Suite 200, St. Paul, MN 55101-3885 USA

© Jack Savage, 2002

All rights reserved. With the exception of quoting
brief passages for the purposes of review, no part
of this publication may be reproduced without
prior written permission from the Publisher.

The information in this book is true and complete
to the best of our knowledge. All recommendations
are made without any guarantee on the part of the
author or Publisher, who also disclaim any liability
incurred in connection with the use of this
data or specific details.

We recognize that some words, model names and
designations, for example, mentioned herein are
the property of the trademark holder. We use them
for identification purposes only. This is not an
official publication.

MBI Publishing Company books are also available
at discounts in bulk quantity for industrial or sales-
promotional use. For details write to Special Sales
Manager at Motorbooks International Wholesalers
& Distributors, Galtier Plaza, 380 Jackson Street,
Suite 200, St. Paul, MN 55101-3885 USA.

Library of Congress Cataloging-in-Publication
Data Available

ISBN 1-7603-1120-X

Edited by Chad Caruthers
Designed by LeAnn Kuhlmann

Printed in China

On the front cover: The beautiful detail of *Miss Scarlett*, a 1951 18-foot Chris-Craft Riviera owned by Robert Rice. *Classic Boating Magazine*

Frontispiece: The 22-foot Sportsman was one of the most popular models in its day. This is the dash of *Mischief*, a 1950 U-22.

On the title page: The Riviera was first introduced in three lengths, 16, 18, and 20 feet. The little 16-footer, such as this 1950 model, could only handle the 60-horsepower Model B engine and seemed sluggish. Consequently, only 174 were built before the 16-foot versions were discontinued after 1951. *Karine N. Rodengen*

On the back cover: **Top left**: The 1958 21-foot Capri Runabout used the same hull as the 21-foot Continental, as well as the same ultra-automotive styling. A raised air scoop on the forward deck ventilated the cockpit. **Top right**: The 1957 Sea Skiff catalog features the 18-foot Open model, which was introduced in 1955. **Bottom left**: Chris-Craft's remarkable Freedom Fleet of 1955 offered the best of American boating life, from the sporting ride of the "rakish" 19-foot Capri Runabout to the entertainment possibilities of the luxury Constellation. **Bottom right**: This 1958 catalog page shows an illustration of the 21-foot Continental.

About the author: Jack Savage is the author of a variety of non-fiction works including *Chris-Craft*, and along with Anthony Mollica he coauthored *Chris-Craft Boats*. An active member of the New Hampshire Antique Boat Museum, Mr. Savage is the owner of Carriage House Publishing and lives near Lake Winnipesaukee, in Middleton, New Hampshire.

R0400629890

BUSINESS/SCIENCE/TECHNOLOGY DIVISION
CHICAGO PUBLIC LIBRARY
400 SOUTH STATE STREET
CHICAGO, ILLINOIS 60605

Contents

Acknowledgments

There would be no classic Chris-Crafts, nor any need for books about them, without the extraordinary enthusiasm and efforts—indeed the obsession—of the thousands of antique- and classic-boat owners who lavish far more time and money than common sense suggests on these glorious reflections of an era past. Thanks to every owner and restorer for making this hobby possible, especially to those whose boats appear in the pages of this modest book.

Individual thanks to Robert Bruce Duncan, Karine Rodengen, Norm and Jim Wangard, and Alan Weitz, all of whom contributed photography far better than my own to these pages. Also to Philip Ballantyne, Chad Caruthers, John deSousa, Mark Evans, Nat Hammond, Jean Hoffman, Bill Irwin and Bruce Wright of Irwin Marine, Kenneth Jorgensen, Jim Murdock, Alan Smith, and Kent O. Smith, all of who, in one way or another, provided me with assistance.

Among the many organizations that are invaluable resources for any researcher are The Mariners' Museum in Newport News, Virginia, home of the Chris-Craft Archives (757) 591-7785; and the Chris-Craft Antique Boat Club (850) 224-2628, overseen by Wilson Wright. Anyone interested in Chris-Craft history should support and make use of them.

Thanks, also, to Anthony Mollica, my friend and coauthor of *Chris-Craft Boats*, whose support for the antique boat hobby is unparalleled. While all of the above have graciously lent me their time and expertise, any errors found in this book are mine alone.

Introduction

In 1949, Chris-Craft, Inc., was a 27-year-old family-owned and operated company. Yes, some marketing promotional materials like to date the company back to the 1870s, when a teenage Christopher Columbus Smith built duck boats with his brother, Hank. However, it wasn't until 1922 that Jay W. Smith, along with his brothers Bernard and Owen and backed by their father Chris' reputation, created the Chris Smith & Sons Boat Company with the goal of mass-producing boats in a way that allowed them to offer extraordinary value for the money—and create speedboats for Every Man.

Yet, 27 years later the company had never experienced an extended, uninterrupted period of growth and expansion. After its remarkable rise from 1922 to 1930, Chris Smith & Sons Boat Company—along with everyone else—endured the years of the Great Depression. From 1937 to 1941 the company rebounded and grew, but its pleasure-boat business came to a complete halt after the Japanese attack on Pearl Harbor on December 7, 1941.

Despite being quick out of the blocks as World War II concluded—the company shipped its first pleasure boat even before the surrender of Japan—an uneven post-war economy and raw material problems held back Chris Smith & Sons Boat Company, as well as other boat builders, into the late 1940s.

Nonetheless, in 1949 the company could legitimately claim to be the largest builder of mahogany boats in the world, offering a full range of runabouts, utilities, and cruisers. The Smiths must have wondered how much more successful they could be without the debilitating interruptions of war and general economic ruin. The 1950s would give them the opportunity to answer that question.

The 1950s were Harsen Smith's decade. His father, Jay W. Smith, turned 65 in 1950, and from the mid-1930s Harsen had been groomed to lead the company. Granted, the growth that Chris-Craft enjoyed in the 1950s was in part driven by the robust economy. Matthews, for example, grew from a one-million dollar company to a fifteen-million dollar company, and Chris-Craft did what it had always done well: recognized opportunities and took advantage of them.

For many, the quintessential 1950s-era Chris-Craft is the Riviera, a double-cockpit runabout that was introduced in 1949 as a direct descendant of the postwar 20-foot Custom. The 18-foot version, such as *Restless*, was the most popular with buyers.

7

By mid-decade, Chris-Craft was at the top of its game and radically reworked the sport boat lineup. Leading the fleet was the Cobra, a single-cockpit speedster based on the venerable 19-foot Racing Runabout and meant to catch the eye of buyers entranced by the latest the Detroit auto industry had to offer, such as the Chevrolet Corvette. *Photo by Classic Boating Magazine*

Prior to World War II and immediately following, runabout-style boats—hulls designed for speed with decked-over engine compartments and individual cockpits—led the sales charge. The 20-foot Custom lured potential boat customers in like a sexy sports car into a car dealership. The reality, though, was that the 20-foot Custom, as influential a model as it was, did not sell all that well—366 units from 1946 to 1949. The Racing Runabout, revered today, sold only 503 units from 1947 to 1954, which was less than half of the 1,040 entry-level SR Rockets sold between 1946 and 1948. The Rocket, though sold as a runabout, was in fact a utility, with the aft passenger open and the engine covered by an engine box. Family boating and water sports would make the more practical utility-style more popular as the 1950s wore on.

Chris-Craft in the 1950s makes a good story, however, because the company's phenomenal growth did not necessarily come easily. Lasting success was constantly challenged by a dynamic and changing marine industry that was destined to leave traditional wooden-planked boats behind. And while the Smiths experienced some of their greatest successes—milestone designs such as the Holiday and the Futura, venerable sellers like the Sportsman and the Constellation, and the launch of the Plywood Boat Division and Sea Skiff Division—they also suffered some of their biggest defeats over the same time period. The Outboard Motor Division flopped, stylish

Although Chris-Craft offered a wide range of styles for its recreational powerboats, from small outboard Kit Boats to Motor Yachts of more than 60 feet, it was the traditional performance-oriented runabouts that defined the mark. The Capri, introduced in 1955, was the last of the wooden runabout models and was forced out after 1961 by the more popular utility-style sport boats. *Classic II* is a 1957 model.

designs like the Cobra and the Silver Arrow sold poorly, and ever less-expensive fiberglass-built upstarts chipped away at Chris-Craft's market share even as the company sold off its all-glass venture, the Lake 'N Sea, as quickly as it had been acquired.

In addition, just as Chris-Craft's power in the marine market peaked, it seemed that the Smiths foretold the fiberglass future of pleasure boats and decided that they wanted no part of it. In fact, as the Eisenhower era came to an end, the Smiths moved the company headquarters to Florida after decades in Algonac, Michigan; installed the first non-Smith as president of the company; and then shocked everyone by selling out to National Automotive Fibers, Inc., in early 1960.

Today, the Chris-Crafts of the 1950s endure as revered classics. For the baby-boom generation, in particular, the two-tone flash of bleached-blonde kingplanks and covering boards evoke memories of childhood water fun. As the family installed itself as the signature of American values, the family utility boat—as big, versatile, and powerful as the American cars that drove us to the lake—replaced the gentleman's runabout as our weekend water warriors. And as much as any boat builder in the world, it was Chris-Craft that designed and built those stylish family boats that combined the warm tradition of solid mahogany with the automotive gloss of 1950s America.

Having established itself as builder of stock runabouts with the 26-foot Chris-Craft in the early 1920s, Chris Smith & Sons introduced its second model, the 22-foot Cadet, in 1927 with bold promises of building as many as 500 units a year—an astounding quantity at the time. The Cadet lasted for three model years. *Morningstar* is a 1928 model that calls Lake Winnipesaukee home.

Chapter One

A Brief History of Chris-Craft

The Smith family of Algonac, Michigan—notably Christopher Columbus Smith—built wooden speedboats for at least two decades before Chris and three of his sons, Jay, Bernard, and Owen, organized the Chris Smith & Sons Boat Company in 1922. Chris, Jay, and Bernard were in fact already world famous among the high-speed racing set, having built and raced record-setting boats for Gar Wood and others.

Unlike their patrons, however, the Smiths were not wealthy and had long been dependent on the few rich men who could afford runabouts. When they sold the family boatyard to Gar Wood in 1922 to finance the new venture, their intent was to build boats that far more Americans could afford. Although they weren't the only boat builders looking to cash in on the "stock boat" phenomenon, the Smiths' timing proved to be ideal.

The Early Days

The Smiths started out with a 26-foot runabout powered by a converted World War I surplus Curtiss OX-5 engine. The boats sold for $3,500. The 26-footer came to be called the Chris-Craft, a name said to be coined by Hamilton Smith and first used on a boat called *Packard Chriscraft*, commissioned and piloted by Colonel Jesse Vincent of Packard Motorcar Co. in the 1922 Gold Cup race.

By the mid-1920s, the nation's economy had recovered, and the Smiths' business started to take off. In 1927 the second standardized runabout model was introduced, a 22-foot Cadet that carried with it bold predictions of 500 units built annually. The Smiths also began building their own engines—the A-70, then the A-120, big V-8s—and launched a dealer network. More important, the company refined its building techniques by implementing assembly-line approaches used successfully in the auto industry and others to streamline the boat-building process. Dividing tasks into individual, repetitive components made it possible to hire unskilled local laborers and train them to do one thing extremely well. As production went up, manufacturing costs went down, as did the sale prices of the boats, which helped expand the market. Before the end of the

The 20-foot postwar Custom Runabout, introduced in 1946 and produced into 1949, established the bleached mahogany two-tone look that defined the 1950s style. *Tahawus* is a 1948 model, shown running on Lake George.

Above: Although the Depression devastated the recreational boating industry, Chris-Craft found ways to survive, and continued to develop and redesign its runabouts. *Four of a Kind* is a 25-foot Custom Runabout that is thought to have been built in 1932 but sold two years later as a 1934 model.

Right: By the early 1940s, Chris-Craft had recovered fully from the Depression and was building the coveted barrelback runabouts, so called because of the pronounced tumblehome aft that created a barrel-shaped transom. *Helen Mary* is a 1941 17-foot Deluxe Runabout.

In the immediate postwar period, quality Philippine mahogany was difficult to come by, and Chris-Craft was forced to use other woods, such as Spanish cedar, in some models. Since the alternative wood did not take a varnished finish as well as mahogany, the hulls were often painted, as on these two Red and White Express Cruisers. Shown are a 1947 23-footer and a 1950 25-footer. The Red and Whites, as these Express Cruisers have come to be known, are extraordinarily popular among collectors. *Karine N. Rodengen*

decade, Chris Smith and Sons legitimately claimed to be the world's largest builder of mahogany boats.

From the beginning, Chris-Craft stock runabouts were V-bottom displacement hulls. The hard-chine V-bottom design was fostered by naval architects such as William Hand Jr. and George Crouch from as far back as the early 1900s and was adopted by any number of boat builders as the best way to handle the heavy, powerful engines of the day. The Smiths often promoted the fact that their boats were built with sturdy double-planked bottoms, with single-plank board-and-batten sides.

The designs of Smith-built boats were typically the product of input from a variety of people and points of view. Chris Smith and long-time Smith employee, Napoleon Lisee, were both influential early on. William "Mac" MacKerer—who ended up working for Chris-Craft for more than 40 years—coordinated much of the design work and helped the Smiths keep close watch on the trends and competition. Chris-Craft's dealer network made it possible for them to aggressively seek out feedback from the market. Perhaps most important to Chris-Craft's success and survival was the fact that the Smiths—starting at the top with Jay W. and Bernard—were experienced boat

Of the 503 19-foot racers built from 1946 through 1954, the first 205 were painted, while the balance featured the classic brightwork as seen on *Fast Forward*, a 1950 model. It featured a split cockpit with a cover for the aft cockpit, and most racers were powered by the 158-horsepower MBL engine that gave it a top speed of 44 miles per hour.

men. They knew what worked, understood the needs and desires of the recreational boating public, and constantly pursued and tested new ideas.

Surviving the Great Depression

Spurred by competition from hundreds of other boat builders, Chris Smith and Sons continued to expand its lineup in the years prior to the Great Depression. In addition to offering its first cruiser, the 38-foot Commuter, the company redesigned the triple-cockpit runabouts, creating a new generation of boats with an upswept deck style. The forward deck rose gradually as it approached the windshield, and louvered vents replaced chrome portholes along the raised

engine compartment, which was also upswept at the rear to mimic the forward deck.

In 1930, as part of a reorganization that was intended to lead to the company going public, the Chris Smith & Sons Boat Company became the Chris-Craft Corporation. The Depression halted those plans, however, as the increasingly dire economic times forced drastic cutbacks. With business savvy and more than a little luck, Chris-Craft would manage to survive. During these perilous times, the Smiths—like other builders—designed and built simpler boats that could be sold for less. Thus, the utility-style boat, featuring an open area aft instead of enclosed cockpits, gained popularity. Not only was it more affordable (at least

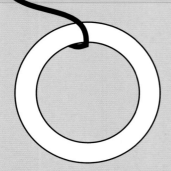

Chris-Craft's Special Touch

How is it that Chris-Craft came to dominate the pleasure-boating horizon during the twentieth century, peaking perhaps during the post–World War II boom of the 1950s? The easy answer, perhaps, is the beauty of the mahogany powerboats the company built. Yet other boat builders turned out boats no less breathtaking.

Chris-Craft thrived not only because it built quality boats, but because it figured out how to build and sell them in quantity. And while Chris-Craft is credited with bringing auto industry style production-line techniques to wooden boat building, the company understood that each boat was special to its owner. Every boat built was assigned a hull number and a hull card—much like a job ticket—where the details of that particular boat were recorded, including dates, materials, colors, and accessories. Those hull cards, for the most part, exist today in the Chris-Craft Collection at the Mariners Museum in Newport News, Virginia. Consequently, today's owners of antique and classic Chris-Craft runabouts, utilities, and cruisers can usually use the hull number stamped on their boats to research the origination of their specific boats.

initially), but the utility had the added advantage of being more practical. Fishermen, families, and fans of watersports found the utilities far easier to use day-in and day-out. Soon, luxury utilities, such as the prewar Sportsman, provided active boaters in the late 1930s with practicality and luxury in equal amounts. Chris-Craft came out of the Depression a stronger company, with an expanded lineup and fewer competitors.

The Late 1930s: Full Speed Ahead

As in the auto industry, speed and performance bring buyers to the sales floor. In 1936, Chris-Craft began marketing its stock Racing Runabouts. In combination with the company's new generation of motors, flathead six-cylinders based on Hercules engine blocks, the Racing Runabouts would pump adrenaline among speed demons for almost 20 years. The Racing Runabout remained a steady seller into the early 1950s, and was transformed into the head-turning Cobra model in 1955.

The late 1930s also saw the ongoing expansion of the cruiser fleet, as Chris-Craft continued its domination of the pleasure-boating business by offering a wide range of stock cruisers. While the company was successful by virtue of building and marketing stock boats, it was possible to order your boat customized to your specifications.

The Riviera models were introduced in 1949 and replaced the 20-foot Custom Runabout. Although the two models appeared similar from a distance, the stock Rivieras featured a single-door engine hatch, fixed windshield, and vinyl upholstery instead of leather, all of which served to make the Riviera less expensive.

Among Chris-Craft's major accomplishments in the 1950s was the launching of the Sea Skiff line of lapstrake boats. Developed to compete with Lyman and other builders of skiffs, the Sea Skiffs used two products the Smiths learned much about while building landing craft for the military during World War II — plywood and Thiokol sealer. *Smith Skiff* is owned today by a member of the Smith family and features a custom burgee design.

The runabouts, however, were still the eye-catching queens of the fleet, and as the 1930s came to a close, Chris-Craft followed the lead of others and jumped into the streamlining craze. Thus were born the so-called barrelbacks, featuring enough tumblehome aft to create a barrel-shaped transom. They were, and are, some of the most prized runabouts ever built, and were among the last triple-cockpit boats offered in the Chris-Craft fleet.

Christopher Columbus Smith, patriarch of the family (though Jay and Bernard had more to do with leading the company to success), passed away in September of 1939. It was, in a variety of ways, a symbol of the end of an era, an era that was brought to a more abrupt close in December 1941 when the bombing of Pearl Harbor brought the United States into World War II and ultimately halted pleasure-boat production for almost four years.

Refocusing in the 1940s

World War II saw Chris-Craft and its employees distinguish themselves as efficient builders of vessels for military use under government contract. The company built landing craft, Navy Pickett boats, 42-foot Command Boats, Army Target boats, and even 60-foot Quartermaster boats. The landing craft, in particular, provided Chris-Craft with experience in marine plywood and Thiokol sealer, both of which would become important as the company expanded its lineup in the 1950s.

As the war ended, Chris-Craft's attention refocused on the recreational market, and the company was well prepped to re-enter the recreational powerboat market—in fact, it shipped its first pleasure boats in July 1945, before the bombing of Hiroshima. However, there were challenges. In the immediate postwar years, Chris-Craft and the rest of the pleasure-boat industry had to overcome the lack of quality,

Chris-Craft-grade Philippine mahogany. Chris-Craft built a number of models out of other types of wood, opting to paint the hulls rather than try to varnish the lesser materials.

A bold new look flowed from the minds of Chris-Craft stylists, creating a sensation in the market that had been starved for new models for four long years. The traditional dark walnut-stained trim that contrasted with the rest of the brightwork was replaced with the bleached-blonde mahogany finish on the kingplanks, covering boards, and cockpit trim. Heralding this new look immediately following the war was the 20-foot Custom Runabout, with its unique convex "bubble" transom and top-of-the-line appointments.

Despite the difficulty in generating growth as the economy shifted from war to peace in the late 1940s, Chris-Craft correctly anticipated the next boom, opening new plants in Caruthersville, Missouri, and Chattanooga, Tennessee. As competition increased from the multitude of outboard boat builders, including the manufacturers of the increasingly popular small fiberglass outboard runabouts, Chris-Craft extended its reach to court more of the market. In 1949 the company launched an outboard motor division, offering first a 5-1/2-horsepower Challenger and subsequently a 10-horsepower Commander. To offer boats that used these outboards, the company started the Kit Boat Division, selling ready-to-assemble plywood runabouts, utilities, and even small pocket cruisers. Chris-Craft's outboard motor division did not find success—patent problems contributed to the company's decision to close the outboard plant. However, the Kit Boats did find buyers among the many young families that wanted to go boating but couldn't yet afford a new Chris-Craft. The Kit Boats evolved into the prebuilt plywood boat division, ultimately known as Cavaliers, that would thrive at the lower end of the market through the 1960s.

As the 1940s came to a close, Chris-Craft was again poised to ride a new boom in recreational boating, this time with Harsen Smith, Jay's son, at the helm.

The Fabulous 1950s

Harsen kept the company focused on maximizing profits through careful control of costs and production. One of Chris-Craft's greatest strengths was its ability to build quality boats relatively quickly and with less expense than the competition. This was as true in the 1920s, when Jay W. announced to the world plans to build some 500 units a year of the Cadet, as it was at the dawn of the 1950s, when the the Smiths introduced the Riviera, a reworked version of the 20-foot Custom that was less expensive to manufacture.

To help keep production costs in line, new models were rarely complete reinventions—many were based on existing hull designs. When the new Cobra replaced the postwar Racing Runabout in 1955, for example, the comparatively radical design featured a fiberglass cowling and vertical dorsal fin. However, the hull of the Cobra was based on the established Racing Runabout.

Also in 1955 the company introduced the Capri runabout to take the place of the Riviera. It would be built in various configurations—including a 21-foot model that shared a hull and the automotive styling cues of the 21-foot Continental—through 1961. Ultimately, the public favored utilities over runabouts, and the Capri was the last true wooden runabout model made by Chris-Craft.

Utilities of the 1950s included the Sportsman, a.k.a. the venerable U-22 (or

The so-called bull-nose bow was prominent on both sport boats and cruisers throughout the 1950s. *Onaway* is a 1957 24-foot cruiser.

19

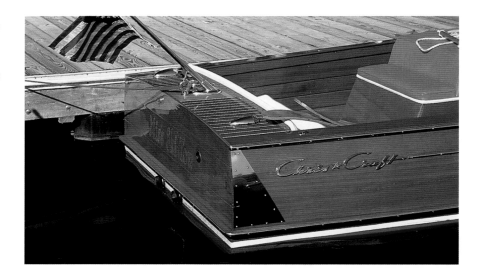

Over the course of the 1950s, the baby boom and the increasing popularity of water sports made the open-hulled utility boats more popular than their decked-over runabout cousins. The 17-foot Ski Boat, such as *Miss Ski Tow*, was introduced in 1959 and featured new V-8 power in the form of a Chevy small block marinized by Chris-Craft.

22-foot utility), which was one of the most popular boats ever sold. Many years later it would be elevated to icon status by virtue of its appearance in the movie *On Golden Pond*. Chris-Craft also launched the Holiday at the beginning of the 1950s, which was then replaced by the Continental in 1955. Throughout this period, utilities continued to usurp the runabouts' reputation for performance and eventually became sport utilities that went fast, worked well for water-skiing, and ultimately dominated the 1960s.

Noting the success of Lyman and other builders of lapstrake skiffs, Chris-Craft launched its own line of lapstrakes, the Sea Skiffs, in 1955. As usually occurred when the Smiths set out to conquer a segment of the market, Sea Skiffs were soon selling as well as any other builder's skiffs. In addition, Chris-Craft bought Roamer, a steel boat company.

As the 1950s came to a close, the company and the industry were changing. Now a large company with factories in Algonac, Holland; Cadillac, Michigan; Chattanooga, Tennessee; Caruthersville, Missouri; and Salisbury, Maryland, the Smiths moved Chris-Craft's headquarters from Algonac to Pompano Beach, Florida, in 1957. Harry Coll was named president, the first non-Smith to hold that position. Fiberglass had made significant inroads, and while Chris-Craft had experimented with the new material in boats like the Silver Arrow (which sported fiberglass from the chine up with a glass-over-wood planked hull), the company was behind other manufacturers in this area. Chris-Craft's Hercules engines had seen their day, and the company began transitioning to a marine version of the small-block 283-ci Chevy. Runabouts, the boats that launched the company, were fading out of fashion. The Smiths felt it was time to cash out.

The 1960s and Beyond
The Smith family sold Chris-Craft in early 1960 to National Automotive Fibers, Inc. (NAFI). Over the course of the next decade, NAFI oversaw the conversion of Chris-Craft from builders of wooden boats to manufacturers of fiberglass boats. While there were a number of outstanding models of wooden Chris-Crafts during the 1960s—sport boats such as the Holiday, Super Sport, and Grand Prix, for example—the end of

In the 1960s, utility-style sport boats were packed with the same kind of horsepower that was wowing car buyers. Brightwork gave way to vinyl, as seen in this 1964 Chris-Craft Super Sport.

the wooden powerboat era was inevitable. Cruisers led the way in fiberglass, with the introduction of the all-glass 38-foot Commander in 1964. The new Chris-Craft owners even launched a fiberglass sailboat, the Motor Sailer, that same year.

The tremendously popular Constellation cruisers, offered in a variety of lengths between 27 and 65 feet, were the longest holdouts of the wooden boats. In 1969, the Connie lineup was whittled to a mere three lengths, and the last recorded wooden Chris-Craft was a 57-footer built at the Holland plant in 1972.

Over the ensuing decades of corporate ownership, there were good years and horrendous years, but Chris-Craft survived it all with its reputation for quality intact: the oil crisis and inflationary 1970s, the buildup and then bankruptcy under ownership by Murray Industries in the 1980s, and the company's sale in 2001, the result of financial problems under the OMC group. In fact, it is a testament to the outstanding workmanship and design of the antique and classic Chris-Crafts that even today, nearly 30 years after the last wooden boat was built, Chris-Craft endures as a symbol of quality.

Chris-Craft

RUNABOUTS · UTILITY BOATS
EXPRESS CRUISERS · CRUISERS · MOTOR YACHTS

Chris-Craft Holiday

WORLD'S LARGEST BUILDERS OF MOTOR BOATS

Luxury was at the center of attention on the black-and-white cover of Chris-Craft's 1951 catalog. After the Great Depression and war years of the 1940s, consumers were ready to embrace pent-up dreams of good living. In the 1950s, Chris-Craft cruisers made those dreams a reality for more Americans than ever.

Chapter Two

1949–1954
Rivieras, Holidays, and Kit Boats

The Chris-Craft story is in many ways the story of the American Dream. Right from the start, the Smith family built its own fortune by selling a dream to the rising middle and upper-middle classes of America. During the 1920s, by helping make the concept of the "stock" powerboat a reality, the Smiths drove boat prices down, created one of the first credit programs, and advertised Chris-Crafts as being accessible for Everyman. In response to the Depression, in the 1930s Chris-Craft added stripped-down utility boats and sold them for as little as $495.

But it wasn't really until the 1950s that Chris-Craft truly made boats for a broad spectrum of the American public. With the increasing reliability of outboard motors, smaller and less expensive craft would gain popularity, as the number of boats in America increased from 2.5 million in 1947 to some 8 million by 1959, when the boat industry was a $2.5 billion industry. As Chris-Craft would learn and then use to its advantage, there was a huge market of young couples that, though not yet ready for a top-of-the-line Chris-Craft, were ready for a less-expensive craft.

Chris-Craft was well prepared to go after these new markets. Although profits were limited by law during the war, Chris-Craft nonetheless emerged in a strong position financially. Its neighbor and long-time competitor, Gar Wood Boats, closed in 1947. Chris-Craft was led by the college-educated son of cofounder Jay W. Smith, Harsen Smith, who represented the third generation of Smiths managing Chris-Craft. Despte wood-supply problems in the years following the war, Chris-Craft booked $14.5 million in sales in 1950 and yielded a profit of $1.5 million.

For beginning boaters, Chris-Craft continued to expand its lineup downward.

It poured millions into the newly established Outboard Engine Division, and then created the Kit Boat Division, which featured a range of do-it-yourself plywood boats. These used Chris-Craft's knowledge gained from building thousands of Higgins-spec landing craft for the military during World War II.

Still, the soul of Chris-Craft would remain within the mahogany-planked runabouts and utilities. By the end of 1949, Chris-Craft was once again able to find supplies of mahogany, and 1950 would be the first postwar year that all runabouts and utilities featured varnished hulls, a welcome contrast to the white-painted cedar hulls of some models in the late 1940s.

The Riviera: The Look of the 1950s

If there was one boat in the Chris-Craft lineup that has come to define the look and style of the 1950s, it is the double-cockpit Riviera runabout

The World's Largest Builders of Motor Boats were exactly that in 1950, when Chris-Craft offered everything from Kit Boats to the newly introduced 62-foot Motor Yacht. It was the beginning of a decade of phenomenal growth for the company, led by Harsen Smith, son of company cofounder Jay W. Smith. Shown on the cover of the 1950 catalog are the Riviera and the 48-foot Double Cabin Flying Bridge Cruiser.

The Rivieras were first introduced in three lengths: 16, 18, and 20 feet. The 18-foot version, like this 1951 model, was the most popular, with 1,210 built from 1949 through 1954. The 16-footer lasted only two model years, with 174 built, while the 20-footer remained in the lineup through 1954, with 288 built.

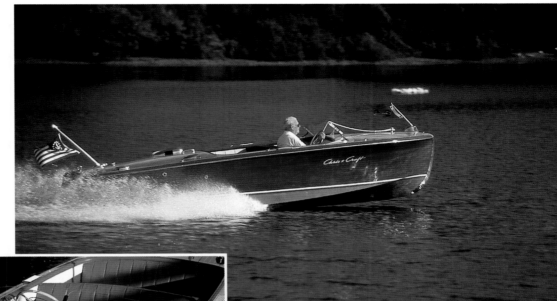

The 18-foot Riviera represented an ideal balance of style, power, and cost for the runabout buyer in the early 1950s. Priced at $2,450, the 18-footer could hit 38 miles per hour when powered by the 131-horsepower KFL engine. *Restless* is a 1950 18-foot Riviera.

that was introduced in 1949 (for the 1950 model year) and remained in production into 1954. Featuring distinctive bleached-blonde mahogany kingplank, engine hatch, and cockpit trim that gave it a flashy two-tone look, the Riviera initially came in three sizes—a 16-footer, an 18-footer, and a 20-footer.

This two-tone look that today defines Chris-Craft in the 1950s had its roots in the 1940s postwar styling of the 20-foot Custom Runabout. Created to continue the elegant legacy of the barrel-back prewar Customs, the 1946 to 1949 20-foot Custom Runabout was the first Chris-Craft to feature the contrasting blonde mahogany kingplank, cockpit trim, and engine hatch cover. The double cockpits forward were luxuriously upholstered in red leather. Hardware included a folding V-shaped windshield with retractable hold-down brackets that was carried over from the last of the prewar Customs.

This styling has been credited to independent designer Don Mortrude, who began working with Chris-Craft in the early 1940s to help create the "dream boats" advertised, but never

Chris-Craft stylist Don Mortrude injected dramatic new flair to the utility lineup with the introduction of the upscale Holiday series for the 1951 model year. The queen of the burgeoning sport boat fleet, the Holiday was a top-of-the-line model that featured teak floors, a built-in bar, and a vast open area aft that was anchored by a large curved rear seat built over a newly designed 40-gallon gas tank, which made it possible to eliminate a rear deck.

Although the 19- and 23-foot Holidays defined the new look of the 1950s-era sport boat, actual sales lagged behind their design influence. The 23-footer sold only eighty-eight units between 1951 and 1953, no surprise given the $5,500-plus price tag. The 19-footer, at around $2,000 less than its big sister, fared better, with 384 built through 1953. *Photo by Classic Boating Magazine*

The Holiday series featured an all-chrome steering column with an automotive-style "on-the-tree" gearshift lever. The instrument panel was mounted below the dash, in front of the driver's knees. *Second Child* is a 1952 19-foot Holiday.

The classic 19-foot Racing Runabout, with its split cockpit and sporting reputation, continued as a steady seller through 1954. It shared some hardware with the Riviera and was most often powered by Chris-Craft's 158-horsepower MBL engine.

built, during the war. Mortrude was steeped in the design world of the nearby Detroit-based automotive industry and had worked with Harley Earl at General Motors. In homage to the top-of-the-line prewar barrelbacks the 20-foot Custom replaced, the hull featured some tumblehome aft, along with a convex "bubble" transom that was raked forward, contrasting smartly with the steeply aft-raked bow and stern poles, both bleached to match the blonde mahogany highlights. The resulting lines suggest a rocket-like profile, a popular shape among the public at the time.

For 1953, Chris-Craft brought back the Rocket moniker (first used in the late 1940s) for this 17-footer based on a square-sterned utility hull. The second-generation Rocket was more of a true runabout than its predecessor, being decked over rather than sporting an engine box. Some 243 Rockets were built in 1953–1954. *Norwegian Wood* is a 1953 model. *Alan Weitz*

The 20-foot Custom was top of the line and was crowned with a price tag to match its status ($4,260 with the 158-horsepower MBL in 1948, or around $1,000 more than a comparably powered Racing Runabout). It was also more time-consuming to build than other models and was produced in modest numbers—366 were built 1946 to 1949.

Although the 20-foot Custom was a great runabout, Chris-Craft had come to dominate the powerboat market by producing good boats for less money than its competitors. By 1949, with the scarcity of quality wood abating somewhat, Chris-Craft morphed the Custom into the Riviera, adding 16- and 18-foot lengths to the lineup and making some design changes that cut the manufacturing cost of the runabout while maintaining the two-tone look.

Although the Riviera looked similar, Chris-Craft had eliminated the Custom's bubble transom, used a single-door engine hatch and a fixed windshield, and typically outfitted the Riviera with vinyl upholstery instead of leather. The result was a boat that looked similar, but could be constructed more easily and sold for less.

The traditionally styled 17-foot double cockpit Deluxe Runabout, which sold some 1,880 units from 1946 into 1950, was discontinued in deference to the 16-foot Riviera—the baby Riv' did not last. It was built to take the four-cylinder, Model B engine, which at 60 horsepower made the boat somewhat underpowered and sluggish. Some 174 were built between 1949 and 1951, when the 16-foot Riviera was discontinued.

The 18-foot Riviera, priced at $2,430, offered the comfort of two amidships cockpits and provided enough performance to claim a 38-miles-per-hour top speed when equipped with the 131-horsepower KFL engine. It was a sales hit. Some 1,210 of the 18-footers were built from 1949 to 1954, four times as many units as the 19-foot split cockpit Racing Runabout during the same period.

The 20-foot Riviera did not do as well as the 18-footer. Just 288 units were made, though unlike the 16-footer, it stayed in the lineup through 1954. Although the 20-footer was listed as a 40-mile-per-hour boat, it may be that customers looking for a larger craft were tempted away by the Holiday utility, which provided a roomier interior. Or perhaps it was too easy to compare the 20-footer to its luxurious older sister, the 20-foot Custom.

The Holiday

The runabouts were not alone in helping define the look of Chris-Crafts in the 1950s. In fact, one of the most significant trends of the decade was the steady move away from the decked-over runabouts toward the more practical, boater-friendly open hulls of the utilities. Beginning with the stylish Holiday in 1950 and continuing with the Continental in 1955 and the Ski Boat in 1959, the utilities would gradually supplant the runabouts as the "sport boats" in the Chris-Craft lineup by providing not only more room for the growing families of the baby-boom era, but also more performance and ease of use for increasingly popular water sports. It was the decade of the family boat.

The queen of the burgeoning sport boat fleet was the Holiday, introduced in 1950 for the 1951 model year in 19- and 23-foot lengths and displacing the luxurious 25-foot Sportsman. The Holiday was to the utility line what the 20-foot Custom was to the runabouts—a style leader that redefined the look of the class. The Holiday was a top-of-the-line model that featured teak floors, a built-in bar, and a vast open area aft anchored by a large curved rear seat built over a newly designed 40-gallon gas tank that made it possible to eliminate a rear deck. Styling cues included a large, steeply raked V-windshield that contributed to a sense of speed, even at the dock. A flush bow cap and rounded covering boards carried the contrasting look of blonde mahogany back to a matching two-tone transom, with blonde spray rails on the sides, suggesting to buyers that it was from the same family as the Riviera. The covering boards were bereft of hardware and contributed to the smooth, streamlined effect. The instrument panel was mounted below the dash near the driver's knees. In a nod to the increasing influence of automotive styling, the gearshift lever was located on the all-chrome steering column.

The 23-foot Holiday was a big boat, with an eight-foot, two-inch beam. And it was expensive. When it was equipped with the powerful and popular 158-horsepower MBL engine, the 23-foot Holiday was credited with 37-mph and listed for more than $5,500. Options included a folding top, fish box, and ice chest. Given its cost, it's no surprise that there were only 88 of the 23-footers built for the 1951–1953 model years.

The new 19-foot Holiday was considerably more affordable—nearly $2,000 less, depending on the engine. For that reason alone, perhaps,

it was more successful on the sales floor, as 384 were built through 1953.

In 1954 the transoms on the Holidays would change from a forward slant to a reverse slant, adding to the overall length of the boats and giving them listed lengths of 20 and 24 feet. Just as with the bubble transom on the 20-foot Custom Runabout, the Holiday's new transom design helped lower the cost of construction. In addition, the instrument panel was returned to a more traditional dashboard location. The 20-footer would continue to outsell its big sister, with 101 built for 1954 compared to 56 units of the 24-footers. Although the Holiday name would return in 1956, it would be on a different hull.

Traditional Styling Survives

Not all of Chris-Craft's sport boats were flashy new designs—there was a market for the more

Although early postwar models were painted, by 1949, the 22-foot Sportsman was finished in traditional brightwork. Available with a variety of engine options, for around $4,000 it could be equipped with the 145-horsepower ML, which gave it a claimed top speed of 36 miles-per-hour. *Mischief* is a 1950 model.

The 22-foot Sportsman offered boaters power, practicality, and payload at a value that made the U-22 one of the most popular models in the lineup. Chris-Craft sold four times as many U-22s as Racing Runabouts from 1946 to 1954. *Karine N. Rodengen*

traditional styling, with plenty of varnish over red mahogany stain. Among the high-profile models in the postwar Chris-Craft lineup was the 19-foot Racing Runabout, a speedy sports car of a boat based on the design of the prewar Racing Runabout. Reintroduced for the 1948 model year, the first 205 units featured painted hulls built using Spanish cedar due to the lack of quality mahogany. By 1950, however, the company was able to re-establish production of this steady seller in all-mahogany with a traditional varnished finish and dark walnut-stained covering boards.

Featuring a split cockpit with the engine amidships, this was not a family boat. The Racing

Above: In addition to the open Sportsman model, the 22-foot hull also sold well in sedan configuration. *Idle-Vice* is a 1953 22-foot Custom Sedan. *Alan Weitz*

Right: Throughout the 1950s, Chris-Craft offered entry-level models so boaters of all means could enjoy a Chris-Craft. To keep costs down on the newly designed 1953 17- and 20-foot Special Sportsman, plywood was used for the inner layer of the double-planked bottom. *Wildfire* is a 1954 17-foot Sportsman.

Runabout was most often sold with the 158 horse-power MBL engine that pushed the speedy craft to a claimed 44-miles-per-hour, though there were also fewer than 100 Racers sold with a 130 horse-power MB, and a few with the 131 horsepower KBL. The Racing Runabout model was a part of the runabout line through 1954, with a total of 503 built between 1947 and 1954. Those sales figures did not make it a top seller, but half a century later, the Racing Runabout is one of the most desirable models among enthusiasts.

For the less well heeled, Chris-Craft offered the 17-foot Special Runabout from 1949 through 1952. Unlike the 17-foot Deluxe Runabout, which was pulled from production in mid-1950, the Special was actually a utility masquerading as a runabout. Based on the 16-foot Special Runabout "Rocket" (which was in turn based on similar prewar models) that sold well immediately following the war, the 17-foot Special Runabout could be fitted with any of the Model K six-cylinder engines, making it far more powerful than the sluggish 16-foot Riviera and its four-cylinder Model B engine. Equipped with the 131-horse-power KBL, the Special was particularly sprightly, earning it a reputation as a sort of "baby racing runabout." It sold 726 units between 1949 and 1952, more than the 19-foot Racing Runabout and 16-foot Riviera combined.

For 1953 the company brought back the Rocket moniker with the 17-foot Rocket Runabout. Based on a square-sterned utility hull, the second generation Rocket was more of a true runabout than its predecessor, being decked over rather than sporting the engine box of its older sister. Like the 17-foot Special Runabout, the Rocket featured a traditional varnished mahogany finish rather than the

Basic in design and featuring minimal flare or tumblehome, flat transoms, and minimal hardware, the Special Sportsmans were nonetheless handsome and reliable boats. They were also bestsellers, with 2,848 of the 17-footers built from 1953 to 1961. *Friend-Ship* is a 1954 17-foot model.

two-tone look. The 17-foot Runabout continued in the lineup through 1958, but it ceased to be called the Rocket after 1954. Some 243 Rockets were built in 1953 and 1954.

The Sportsman

Better known to the public as a quintessential Chris-Craft of the period was the Sportsman line of utilities. Given that the designs were proven and used less wood to build than any of the runabouts or cruisers, the Sportsman was among the first off the line when pleasure-boat production was restored in mid-summer of 1945, and it would continue in various lengths and configurations through 1954. Based on prewar designs going back to 1934, the 18-foot, 22-foot, and 25-foot Sportsman models received modest styling updates for the postwar generations. The bow

and covering boards were rolled and rounded with a bow cap, giving the boats a softened look.

At the forefront of the Sportsman fleet initially following the war was the 25-footer, which was based on the prewar 25-foot Sportsman and continued the tradition of a high-dollar luxury utility. It was dropped in 1950 in favor of the 23-foot Holiday that was introduced for 1951.

The Sportsman that even the non-boater recognizes today, thanks in large part to the movie *On Golden Pond*, is the 22-footer known commonly as the U-22 (from its hull number). This 22-foot Sportsman was based on the prewar 22-foot Deluxe Utility. Like Express Cruisers, Racing Runabouts, and some other models in the 1946 to 1948 period, many hulls were built using cedar planking and painted instead of varnished. By 1949, and through 1954, the 22-foot Sportsman was

Cruising in a Chris-Craft didn't necessarily mean owning a floating palace — Express Cruisers were popular models in the lineup. *Comfy* is a 1950 28-footer on Lake Winnipesaukee, in New Hampshire. The *MS Mount Washington* is in the background.

finished in traditional brightwork and was available with a variety of engine options, including the 145-horsepower ML, which gave it a claimed 36-miles-per-hour top speed and sold for around $4,000. Practical, fast enough for most boaters, and able to carry cargos of fishermen or families, the U-22 proved its popularity by selling more than 2,000 units from 1946 through 1954. Another 436 of the same hull were built and sold as 22-foot Custom Sedans, which featured streamlined hardtops.

The 18-foot Sportsman appeared in name in 1949 and lasted through 1954, though the boat was previously sold as the 18-foot Deluxe Utility between 1946 and 1948. It was offered with a Model B or Model K engine and sold for around $1,000 less than the U-22, depending on the engine and options. Some 1,186 of the 18-footers were built.

In 1950, Chris-Craft lengthened the smallest of the Sportsman line, the 16-footer, to 17 feet. Traditionally styled, it was a direct descendant of

At the dawn of the new decade in 1950, Chris-Craft offered twenty-seven different cruiser styles in sixteen hull-lengths, from 21 to 62 feet. Even the smaller cruisers provided a surprising amount of room for entertaining friends. *Friendship* is a 1950-model 30-foot Express Cruiser.

the 15-1/2-foot utility first offered during the depths of the Depression. Powered by the four-cylinder Model B engine, it was a practical boat for the cost-conscious, and 260 were built through 1952.

In 1953, in order to bring lower-priced Sportsman models to market, Chris-Craft introduced the newly designed 17- and 20-foot Special Sportsman utilities. Among the cost-saving features was the use of plywood for the inner layer of the traditional Chris-Craft "double-planked"

bottom. The Special Sportsman models featured none of the flair of the flashy Holiday—transoms were flat, the sides minimized flare and tumble-home, and hardware was minimal. The 20-foot Special Sportsman featured an optional third seat in front of the engine box.

The entry-level Special Sportsman models would last into 1961, when the growing plywood Cavalier value line forced them out. Nonetheless, based on units sold, the Specials were the most popular models of the Chris-Craft lineup, with

Above: The Commander was introduced in 1949, graced with postwar styling courtesy of Don Mortrude. By 1953, when this 35-foot Commander model came off the line, Chris-Craft was battling with competitors such as Owens, Mathews, and Richardson for the cruiser market. *Karine N. Rodengen*

Left: The Commander was offered in hardtop or open flybridge configurations and had an impressive top speed of 29 miles per hour when equipped with twin engines. It was a mainstay of the small cruiser market for a number of years. *Myst'ere* is a 1954 36-foot model. The 36-footer shared its hull with the Corvette model. *Alan Weitz*

2,848 17-footers sold from 1953 to 1961 and another 476 of the 20-footers sold as well.

Cruisers

Cruisers had long been part of the mix of boats coming out of the Smiths' Algonac shop—records indicate that they built some custom cruisers even before the days of Chris-Craft stock boats in the 1920s. But when the company launched its first stock cruiser, the 38-foot Commuter, in 1929, the development of the cruiser lineup was hindered by the Depression and put off until later in the 1930s. Just as stock cruiser offerings had peaked at twenty-one models varying in length from 23 to 55 feet in 1941, the war brought pleasure boat production to a halt. In 1945, when Chris-Craft could again turn its attention to recreational boating, the shortages of quality wood that plagued the runabouts also played havoc with Chris-Craft's desire to expand its cruiser lineup. The dream-boat designs coming off the stylists' drawing boards during the war had to wait.

By 1949, Chris-Craft was feeling bullish enough to expand the catalog of stock cruisers to 25 different models, almost doubling the offerings available in 1948. Among the new models were those both at the bottom and at the top of the lineup: the 21-foot Express Cruiser (introduced as a copycat of the Cruise Along), which sold for around $2,700 and the 52-foot Conqueror Motor Yacht, which, when powered by twin 200-horsepower GM diesels, sold for just shy of $50,000. Also introduced in 1949 was the 34-foot Commander, which featured styling from the pen of independent designer Don Mortrude layered over the basic design of the prewar Conqueror cruiser. The Commander was offered in hardtop or open flybridge configurations, could reach 29-mph when equipped with twin engines, and sold for $13,200, depending on options. It would go on to be a mainstay of the small cruiser market for a number of years.

As the new decade rolled around, Chris-Craft upped the cruiser ante by adding a new 62-foot Motor Yacht. With a beam of 16 feet, the big boat could sleep thirteen and had four toilets, including two with showers. The 62-footer listed for $98,000 in stock trim, almost double the cost of its smaller sister boat, the 52-foot Motor Yacht. The 52-footer featured a stem that curved forward before wrapping back into a large bow cap, which was a precursor to the so-called bull-nose bow that could also be seen on the Holiday in 1951 and was prevalent throughout the lineup in the 1950s.

In 1951 and 1952, Chris-Craft added the 47-foot Buccaneer and the 50-foot Catalina to the lineup, as the Korean War kept changes relatively subtle among cruisers. In 1953 the catalog stayed steady with twenty-seven models, including a 33-foot Capitan (a Sedan Express cruiser), a 40-foot Express Cruiser, and the 52-foot Conqueror. The smaller Motor Yacht was stretched to list at 55 feet, and the biggest boat in the fleet went to 63 feet.

The lineup of the mid-1950s peaked in 1954 with the introduction of the 35-foot Sport Fisherman, the 36-foot Corvette (sharing the Commander hull), and the 45-foot Corsair. With the Sport Fisherman, as it had with any number of models in the past, Chris-Craft was looking to capitalize on a style dominated up to then by smaller boat builders. It featured painted (rather than varnished) cabin sides, ample side decks, and dual controls—including those on the fishing bridge. Powered by twin diesels, it sold for around $27,000, depending on options. The 45-foot Corsair had an additional foot of beam compared to the 45-foot Double Cabin Flying Bridge cruiser, which made it possible to add walk-around decks. The massive bow cap that had been the signature of Chris-Craft's postwar cruisers was tossed in favor of a more light-handed stem treatment.

Air Rescue Boat

Chris-Craft was well versed in the ways of the U.S. military, having built thousands of boats—including more than 10,000 plywood landing craft—during World War II. So it was logical that the company would be interested and willing to work with the government during the Korean conflict in the early 1950s.

The task at hand was to design and build an Air Rescue Boat that could be used to pull downed airmen out of the ocean. It was meant to be a combination water ambulance, with a sick bay to attend to the injured, and fire boat, capable of pumping streams of seawater onto flaming wreckage while rescue personnel saved survivors.

Chris-Craft designers generated two examples of a clever prototype that included a transom ramp that could be lowered to allow pilots to be brought onboard at water level rather than being heaved over the side. An underwater cage surrounded the screws to keep personnel who were in the water at the stern from being injured.

The boat never went into production, however. Faced with a government bureaucracy that repeatedly and frequently changed the design specs without offering up additional compensation, Chris-Craft ultimately decided that the potential contract wasn't worth the effort. Although the company frequently assisted the government when asked, it declined further government contracts.

The New Boaters

Even as Chris-Craft revamped its lineup of stock mahogany runabouts, utilities, and cruisers, expanding downward with the Special Sportsman and upward with the 62-foot Motor Yacht, the company recognized a new market opportunity among the legions of entry-level boaters. Among the increasing millions of boats registered, many were outboard car-toppers and trailer boats owned by young war veterans and others looking for an inexpensive way onto their local lakes.

The entry-level market was important to Chris-Craft for a variety of reasons. First and foremost, the company needed to protect its market share. Small fiberglass boats were not yet a challenge in 1950, but companies such as Lyman were poised to take advantage of the increasing reliability of outboard engines. Second, Chris-Craft had learned that it was important to build brand loyalty right from the start, and if a new boater could only afford a small outboard, it behooved the Smiths to make sure it was a Chris-Craft. Then, when it came time for that boater to step up the boating ladder, a Chris-Craft inboard would be his first choice. Third, outboard engines and boats could be sold outside of traditional marinas and boat dealers, thus expanding Chris-Craft's potential sales outlets.

In order to go after the outboard market, Chris-Craft needed two things: outboard motors and boats to hang them on. It would develop and offer both.

Outboard Engines

Any time Chris-Craft considered taking on a new part of the market, the company started by sizing up the competition. Chris-Craft would dissect the product and then try to figure out ways to not only improve on it, but how to also manufacture it for less money and sell it for a lower price. The strategy of the Outboard Engine Division was no different.

When it came to outboard engines, company marketing executives determined that a five-horsepower unit would be the most popular. They wanted an engine that would be convenient to service, in part because it would then lend itself to further development. Jay W. Smith was reportedly heavily involved in the development

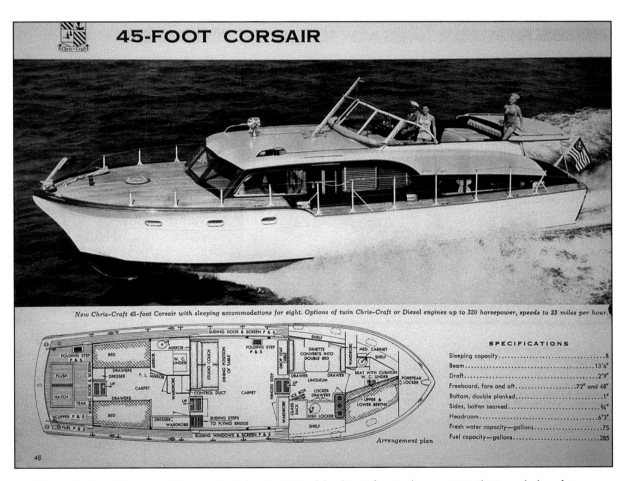

45-FOOT CORSAIR

New Chris-Craft 45-foot Corsair with sleeping accommodations for eight. Options of twin Chris-Craft or Diesel engines up to 320 horsepower, speeds to 23 miles per hour.

SPECIFICATIONS

Sleeping capacity	8
Beam	13'6"
Draft	2'9"
Freeboard, fore and aft	72" and 48"
Bottom, double planked	1"
Sides, batten seamed	¾"
Headroom	6'3"
Fresh water capacity—gallons	75
Fuel capacity—gallons	285

Arrangement plan

48

In addition to the Sport Fisherman and Corvette, the 45-foot Corsair joined the Chris-Craft cruiser lineup in 1954. The Corsair had one foot more beam than the 45-foot Double Cabin Flying Bridge cruiser, making it possible to add walk-around decks.

SHOWBOATS for 1954

Chris-Craft

WORLD'S LARGEST BUILDERS OF MOTOR BOATS

Chris-Craft brought color back to the sales catalog in 1954 for the launch of three new cruiser models. Featured on the cover is the 45-foot Corsair.

of the engine, as was Harry Coll, a college friend of Harsen's who would be named manager of the new outboard plant in Grand Rapids, Michigan.

In 1949, after eight years of development, Chris-Craft introduced its first outboard, the 5-1/2-horsepower Challenger two-stroke alternate-firing twin with full reverse. With bore and stroke of 2 x 1-1/2 inches, it displaced 9.42 ci, weighed 46 pounds, carried 1-1/2 gallons of fuel, and offered a gear ratio of 14:25. Jay W. was determined to improve on the standard magnetos and carburetion of the day.

But one motor did not an outboard division make. A year later, Chris-Craft introduced the 10-horsepower Commander outboard. Like its little brother, the Commander was an alternate-firing two-cylinder two-stroke, with bore and stroke of 2-1/2 x 2-1/32 inches displacing 19.94 inches and weighing 72 pounds. Fuel capacity was 2 gallons.

Next on the agenda was a fleet of inexpensive outboard boats. Double-planked mahogany hulls are heavy and thus were not good candidates to be the foundation of a line of outboards. But

Chris-Craft did have four years of experience building boats with plywood during the war, and small plywood craft would make excellent cost-effective outboards.

As the story goes, a few small boats were needed in order to test the new outboard engines in real-world conditions during development. That task apparently fell to Bernard Smith's son, George, who built some small utility-class stock outboard racing hulls for the purpose. A stretched version of one of those 13-foot test boats is said to have become the 14-foot Kit Boat that was offered to the public in late 1950. And so was launched the Kit Boat Division of Chris-Craft.

What better way to keep prices down than to eliminate much of the labor involved in constructing the boat? Consumers could order a variety of small boats that would arrive in a box full of precut pieces for assembly at home. Chris-Craft offered three models in mid-1950: an 8-foot Pram, a 14-foot Rowboat, and a 14-foot Outboard Kit Boat. The company sought out the new do-it-yourself boaters through the magazines that catered to them—*Popular Mechanics*, for example. The kits were also marketed as projects appropriate for kids—fathers and sons—through ads in magazines like *Boys' Life*.

In 1951, Chris-Craft expanded the Kit-Boat lineup by adding a 12-foot Runabout Boat Kit to go with the 14-foot Runabout, as well as a Sailing Kit for the 8-foot Pram. But the plan called for more than just outboards, as Chris-Craft began to offer kits for substantially larger boats designed to use inboard engines. An 18-foot Outboard Express Cruiser Boat Kit could be configured to use outboard or inboard power, and there was a 21-foot Sportsman Boat Kit that traded on the popularity of the Sportsman in the standard Chris-Craft lineup, with a 21-foot Express Cruiser Boat Kit built on the same basic hull. Buyers purchased the 21-foot hull Kit, then

could customize their boats with the Sportsman Windshield Kit, the Sportsman Pilot Seat Kit, the Express Cruiser Cabin Kit, and/or the Express Cruiser Flying Bridge Windshield Kit. The Sportsman went for $614; the Express Cruiser for $747, plus engine. The kits included decals, with "Kit Boat" included underneath the Chris-Craft logo.

Chris-Craft also offered in 1951 a 31-foot Express Cruiser Boat Kit, which, unlike the rest of the Kits, featured a double-planked bottom (1/2-inch mahogany planks over 1/4-inch plywood) to go with the 1/2-inch fir marine-plywood sides. The do-it-yourselfers were also provided with the traditional canvas and bedding compound Chris-Craft liked to use between the bottom layers. The deck was canvas over plywood, and the covering boards and cabin front and sides were Philippine mahogany. The cabin could accommodate a dinette, galley, toilet, and two berths. The shipping weight of the complete Kit was 5,000 pounds, and it sold for $1,995 (without the engine)—compared to around $10,000 for the 31-foot standard Chris-Craft Express Cruiser, power included.

Meanwhile, the outboard engines proved to be fast and reliable, and sales brochures urged consumers to "Try 'em! Troll 'em! Clock 'em!" The early Kit Boat catalogs featured pictures of completed boats motoring along courtesy of Chris-Craft Challenger and Commander outboards on the transoms. Alan and Silvia Smith, two of Bernard Smith's grandchildren, were active in the Algonac Boat Racing Association, using the Challenger and Commander outboards with success in the B and M hydroplane classes. Chris-Craft subsequently offered a 10-foot Utility Racing Pram Kit. It was no hydro, but as the brochure made sure to point out, "With the addition of a trunk deck, steering wheel, and throttle, the hull will meet Class JU, AU, and BU specifications under the current rules of the

American Power Boat Association." Overall, the build-at-home boats found enough of a market that in 1952 the company established the Kit Boat Division of Chris-Craft.

But then came problems. After investing more than $1 million, the outboard engine program was shut down in 1953 and the doors were locked on the Grand Rapids plant. Explanations for the rather abrupt halt of outboard production ranged from the claim that the rest of the boating lines demanded all of the Smiths' attention to the suggestion that they had concluded that success in the outboard business would require a full lineup of motors—which the company wasn't prepared to follow through on.

There were also charges of patent infringements from a competing manufacturer. The lower unit on the Challenger motor used a bearing that violated a patent held by Mercury, and there were also potential patent problems with the reed plate design and a few other items. Carl Kiekhaefer sued Chris-Craft. The 5-1/2-horsepower Challenger, which did not have the same patent problems as the Commander, was produced for another 10 years under license in England and elsewhere.

The shutdown—a difficult decision no doubt—was likely due to a combination of factors. Sales of the engines may have been below projections, and development costs for new engines were likely substantial. Add bitter competition, marginal profit potential, and a lawsuit, and the Smiths probably decided that there were bigger fish to fry in the recreational boating

Correctly predicting the rise in popularity of small outboard boats, Chris-Craft created the Kit Boat Division in 1950. The Kits, such as this 1952 14-foot Deluxe Runabout, were not only fun projects but handy craft for one of Chris-Craft's new outboard motors, like this 5-1/2-horsepower Challenger.

pond. In fact, Chris-Craft would turn around and immediately begin development of the new lapstrake boat division, Sea Skiff.

The tribulations with the outboard engines did not slow the growth of the Kit Boat Division, however. In 1953, the expanded lineup included twenty models in ten lengths ranging from the 8-foot Pram to the 31-foot Express Cruiser. Included was a 12-foot Penguin Sailing Dinghy Boat Kit that met the competition specifications of the Penguin Class Dinghy Association. It featured a plywood rudder and centerboard and spruce mast and boom, and was designed to carry 72 square feet of sail. As with other Kits, the shipping crate was designed to double as a building jig. Also new was a 14-foot Duckboat Kit, a plywood version of the kind of craft Chris Smith built early in his career.

Having successfully established direct mail sales of the Kit Boats as well as sales through hardware stores and lumberyards, Chris-Craft introduced a few non-boat kits as well. The knotty pine Chris-Craft Gun Cabinet could store your hunting weaponry when you weren't out in your Duckboat, and the knotty pine Chris-Craft Treasure Chest also doubled as a bench seat.

Less successful was the 14-foot Land Cruiser mobile-home kit introduced in 1954 and dropped a year later. The Land Cruiser was likely an outgrowth of the Chris-Craft

The 5-1/2 horsepower Challenger outboard was a two-stroke alternate-firing twin with full reverse. With bore and stroke of 2 x 1-1/2 inches, it displaced 9.42ci, weighed 46 pounds, carried 1-1/2 gallons of fuel, and offered a gear ratio of 14:25. The Challenger did not have patent problems as the 10-horsepower Commander did and consequently was produced under license for 10 years after the shutdown of the Outboard Division.

Lifetime Boat Trailers, sold as handy add-ons to haul your Kit Boat to water once it was built. There were four trailer models: CC-300, CC-650, CC-1000, and CC-2200, the model numbers corresponding to the trailers' capacities.

Chris-Craft 14-ft. De Luxe Runabout Kit Boat—fast, stable, maneuverable! Complete kit only $162. Standard model also available, only $149. Great buys! Act NOW!

14-ft. De Luxe Runabout Kit,* shown above.

NOW! Own a CHRIS-CRAFT
for as little as $42 full price!

Assemble a new Chris-Craft Boat Kit! Have fun doing it! SAVE ½ or more! They're a cinch to put together! *Only the finest materials available are included in each Chris-Craft Kit: accurately precut Philippine Mahogany parts and Fir marine-plywood panels; brass fastenings; special screw driver; seam compound; decals. Illustrated instructions make assembly EASY with household tools! New Chris-Craft Boat Kits are the greatest values ever offered in the history of the boating industry! Thousands are assembling 'em! HURRY! Buy your Chris-Craft Boat Kit NOW! Mail coupon for FREE folder TODAY!
(Kit prices quoted f.o.b. factory, subject to change without notice.)

Dandy 8-ft. Pram Kit Boat. Assemble it yourself for fishing and fun! Kit price only $42. Pram Sail Kit also available, $65.

Fast 12-ft. Runabout Kit Boat—easy to assemble! V-bottom. Sturdy but lightweight for car-top carrying. BIG value at $118.

Rugged 14-ft. Fishing Skiff Kit priced at $111, complete! You can't go wrong! Don't delay! Buy your Chris-Craft Boat Kit today.

$595 buys a kit for this new 18-ft. Outboard Express Cruiser! Tremendous savings! Outboard or inboard power. Truly a beauty!

Big 21-ft. Sportsman Kit Boat with roomy cockpit. A terrific kit buy at $614. Get complete data on all kits. Mail coupon today!

Beautiful 21-ft. Express Cruiser Kit Boat brings real cruising pleasure down to rock-bottom price! This kit sells for only $747. Act NOW!

Save thousands of dollars! Buy kit for this sleek 31-ft. Express Cruiser at $1995, full price! Mail coupon for FREE Kit Folder NOW!

10 h. p.

5½ h. p.

THE CHOICE OF EXPERTS
Two great Chris-Craft Outboard Motors—5½ and 10 h.p.—the choice of experts! New dependability, all-around performance! For every outboard need, buy Chris-Craft!

Chris★Craft
CHRIS-CRAFT CORPORATION, ALGONAC, MICH.
MOTOR BOATS • MARINE ENGINES • OUTBOARD MOTORS • BOAT KITS
WORLD'S LARGEST BUILDERS OF MOTOR BOATS

CHRIS-CRAFT CORPORATION, Algonac, Mich.
Send me FREE folder on:
☐ Chris-Craft Boat Kits   ☐ Chris-Craft Outboard Motors
Name
Address
City _____ Zone _____ State

Chris-Craft's Kit Boats were inexpensive and came precut and ready to assemble, as shown in this magazine ad. The shipping crate was used as the cradle during construction. For many, they were an irresistible way to acquire a "real" Chris-Craft. The lineup included more than just small outboards, ranging from the 8-foot Pram to the 31-foot Express Cruiser, which sold for $1,995.

Looking Ahead

Although Chris-Craft had experienced some failures in the early 1950s, by 1954 the company was preparing for its next assault on the recreational boating market. The automotive industry, powered by a thriving advertising media in both magazines and increasingly, television, was creating new looks and expectations among its American consumers. It was time to revamp the oldest designs and create bold, new styling that reflected the dreams of the boating public during the days of Eisenhower.

Only 106 Cobras were built during its one model year, including fifty-one 18-footers and fifty-five 21-footers. Most 18-footers used the 131-horsepower KBL, which gave them a top speed of 39 miles per hour. *Photo by Classic Boating Magazine*

Chapter Three

1955
The Cobra Strikes

Chris-Craft was busy in the years leading up to 1955, a year that represented what *Motor Boating* magazine called "the biggest and most important model changeover in the history of the company." Granted, those same words were often written about Chris-Craft, but this time it was never more true. Not only were the traditionally built sport boats and cruisers revamped and updated for the 1955 model year but during the same period, Chris-Craft launched the lapstrake Sea Skiff Division, established the Plywood Boat Division, and purchased Roamer, a company that built steel-hulled Cruisers. It was arguably the peak of Chris-Craft in terms of activity, design, and market influence. Although sales were higher in subsequent years, Chris-Craft never again saw its lineup revamped in such a major way under the 40-year reign of the Smith family.

Their timing was ideal. Unemployment was as low as 4.2 percent in the mid-1950s. Personal income doubled during the decade, and purchasing power increased by 30 percent. Ray Kroc opened his first McDonald's restaurant in Des Plaines, Illinois, in 1955, and Disney opened Disneyland in Anaheim, California. Consumer culture, led by the nation's first credit card in 1950, was in full swing. In 1955, Americans bought 7.9 million new automobiles, four times as many as just nine years before.

America's materialistic nature was a boon to boating. A *Motor Boating* survey estimated that by 1955, there were between five and six million pleasure boats in the United States, or one for every thirty-two people in the country. This represented a doubling of boats in just six years. Among those, one million were inboards.

New Look Runabouts

Sports cars were all the rage in the mid-1950s, and when Chevrolet unveiled a prototype two-seater in 1952, response from the car-crazy public was so strong that Chevrolet rushed it into production. In 1953 the first Corvettes came off the line, sporting fiberglass bodywork. Although sales of the Corvette were sluggish at the start, the unveiling of Ford's Thunderbird shortly thereafter kept the American sports car phenomenon going and kept customers flocking to the

The Cobra was a radical departure for Chris-Craft—a sporty single-cockpit boat with a dorsal cowling and vertical tail fin constructed from fiberglass, the first substantive use of the new material by the company. The appearance of the Cobra meant the return to V-8 power in the Chris-Craft lineup, as marinized versions of the Chrysler Hemi and a Cadillac V-8 were options on the 21-foot version. *Karine N. Rodengen*

In 1955 Chris-Craft introduced a blockbuster lineup it called the Freedom Fleet. The Cobra (top right) replaced the Racing Runabout it was based upon, and the Continental (top left) replaced the Holiday as the queen of the luxury utility fleet. The Constellation cruiser (middle) was a classic model that would remain in production until the bitter end of wooden Chris-Crafts in 1972. The sleek Capitan is below.

1955 FREEDOM FLEET

Chris ☆ Craft

WORLD'S LARGEST BUILDERS OF MOTOR BOATS

showrooms—even if they ended up purchasing more practical models once they got there.

Meanwhile, Chris-Craft's own sports car of the waterways, the Racing Runabout, was due for a redesign, and the company wanted a flashy lead model to bring customers into the nationwide network of Chris-Craft dealerships. Working off the hull of the 19-foot Racer, Chris-Craft designers developed what would be one of the most radical designs ever to come out of Algonac—the Cobra.

The Cobra's most distinctive feature was a single vertical dorsal reminiscent of the Ventnor Runabouts of a decade before. The fin and deck lid were finished in a golden hue and—remarkably for the wooden boat men of Chris-Craft—fashioned out of fiberglass, which was better suited for the complex shapes. Chris-Craft had been using fiberglass in some hidden parts of cruiser cabin interiors, but the Cobra represented the company's first notable use of the new material. The rest of the Cobra runabout was built in a traditional Chris-Craft fashion—a somewhat time-consuming task given the lines of the boat.

Other changes in 1955 saw the Capri Runabouts, in 19- and 21-foot lengths, replace the venerable Riviera. They sported the mid-1950s wrap-around windshield. *Photo by Classic Boating Magazine*

The Cobra featured the blonde kingplank that marked most of the contemporary Runabouts, as well as a raked stem with a bull-nose bow. Hardware was shared with the Capri runabout, which was introduced that same year to replace the Riviera. Offered in 21-foot and 18-foot versions and featuring a single cockpit, the foredeck of the 21-foot Cobra was a beamy 8 inches wider than its Racing Runabout predecessor, which gave it a look some say mimics the three-point hydroplanes of its time. As *Motor Boating* noted, "[Cobras] are distinguished by bows that lean ahead, sheer lines that taper close to the water at the transom, curved swept-back windshields, lavishly appointed cockpits, raised engine cowls, graceful tailfins and an abundance of speed."

Rare at the time and considered a flashy classic decades later, the Cobra was an expensive but powerful boat. Only 106 were built, including fifty-one 18-footers and fifty-five 21-footers, and it was offered for only one model year. The shorter versions retailed from $3,710 to $3,950 depending on the engine option—most were

Above: Following in the tradition of the 25-foot Sportsman and the 1951–1954 Holiday Series, the 1955 Continental offered top-of-the-line luxury in a utility-style sport boat. In contrast to the curved windshields on the new runabouts, the Continental used a steeply raked flat windshield. *Best Revenge* is a 1955 25-foot Continental.

Left: The Continentals were offered in four lengths: 18, 20, 22, and 25 feet. They shared hulls with the more affordable Holiday Series. This 20-footer was the thirty-fourth of its kind in 1955 and was powered by a 145-horsepower ML engine.

The smaller Continentals, such as this 18-footer, seated six comfortably. *Smyrna* is a 1955 model.

shipped with the 131-horsepower KBL that pushed the 18-footer to 39 miles per hour. The 21-foot model topped out at $6,560 when powered by the 285-horsepower V-8 Cadillac engine that gave it a claimed 50 to 55 miles per hour, and eighteen went out the door so equipped. Some twenty-one proud new big-Cobra owners opted instead for the 200-horsepower Chrysler Hemi at $5,690, while the balance of the 21-footers sported the 158-horsepower MBL, the engine used in the 19-foot Racing Runabout that the Cobra replaced.

The other new runabout in the 1955 Freedom Fleet, the Capri, would last six years, with slight modifications during that time. It would also be the last of the traditional wooden runabouts. Offered initially in 19- and 21-foot versions, the Capri replaced the six-year-old Riviera model.

The early Capris followed in the tradition of the two-toned look that began with the postwar 20-foot Custom Runabout in 1946 and continued in the Rivieras. Like its ancestors, the 1955–56 Capri featured bleached mahogany kingplank, cockpit trim, and engine hatch. A wraparound windshield modernized and streamlined the look.

The 19-footer could be ordered with a choice of K-series engines, ranging from the 95-horsepower K (33 miles per hour) to the 131-horsepower KBL (38 miles per hour), with prices starting at $3,390 and going up to $3,630. The smaller Capri met with reasonable sales success, as 786 found homes between 1955 and 1958—numbers comparable to the sales levels of the 18-foot Riviera, for example.

The 21-foot Capri featured not only the more powerful M-series engines, including the 158 horsepower MBL (41 miles per hour for $4,280), but also the 200-horsepower Chrysler Hemi V-8 (44 to 49 miles per hour for $5,290). The double-cockpit Capri could carry six adults comfortably, and sold for $300 to $400 less than a similarly powered single-cockpit Cobra. In 1956 buyers of the 21-foot Capri could order their boats stuffed with the 285-horsepower Cadillac V-8. The 1955–1956 Capri was replaced in 1957, after a total of 170 units went out the door.

Continental Concept

Although all eyes in 1955 may have been on the sexy Cobra, consumers proved more willing to reach into their wallets for utility models. Still, the 18- and 22-foot Sportsman models were, like the Racing Runabout, aging designs, and Chris-Craft mothballed them. Gone, too, was the luxurious Holiday model of 1951 to 1954. Instead, at the top-of-the line in the utility sport

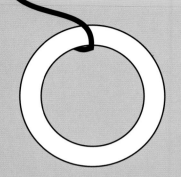

Chris-O-Matic Transmission

Among the innovations from Chris-Craft in the mid-1950s was an automatic transmission, which it dubbed the "Chris-O-Matic," with electric-hydraulic clutch control. As the automotive industry developed, installed, and promoted automatic transmissions, boating customers expected the same convenience.

The Chris-O-Matic was offered as an option on all Chris-Craft engines except the four-cylinder Models A and B, and could be retrofitted. As described in *Motor Boating*, "Chris-O-Matic, a new marine innovation which actually shifts the gears for the skipper, is available for all but the 60hp series. With this new electric-hydraulic shifting mechanism, the man at the wheel simply flips a selector, much as he would flip a light switch, and instantaneously an electric motor pumps hydraulic fluid into a cylinder to actuate a piston, which then accomplishes the desired shift. This control, designed for Chris-Craft engines, can be installed on most engines already in operation. It can also be hooked up for dual control installations."

boat fleet for 1955 was the new Continental series, offered in four hull lengths: 18, 20, 22, and 25 feet. The Continentals shared hulls and bull-nose bow styling with what the Chris-Craft catalog called the Holiday series (the Holiday name had been relegated to second-string status, the "Holiday series" retailing for about $500 less than comparably powered Continentals of the same length). The Continentals continued with the two-tone styling highlighted by blonde king-plank, cockpit trim, and aft deck, and in contrast to the curved windshields on the new runabouts, the Continental and Holiday series utilities sported a raked flat windshield. The smaller mod-els could seat six, while the 25-footer added a three-quarter amidships seat for added passenger payload (ten). Marketing copy promoted the "outward flaring hull sides that increase the beam and promote a drier ride" (the beam on the 22-footer, for example, was an impressive 7 feet, 11-3/4 inches). The 25-footer could be equipped with twin six-cylinder engines, which brought the price to a hefty $7,000.

In 1956 the 22- and 25-foot Continentals were stretched slightly, becoming 23 and 26 feet, respectively. Ditto the 22-foot Holiday series version of the hull, while the 25-foot Holiday series was dropped from the lineup.

Previous page: Even as Chris-Craft designers continually revamped the flashy sport boats, the tried-and-true designs continued to sell steadily to those boaters wanting a more traditional (and less expensive) Chris-Craft. *Harvey J* is a 1956 17-foot Runabout, one of ninety-four square-sterned 17-footers built between 1955 and 1956. This model was one of the last to feature the V-windshields.

Seventeen Feet of Tradition

Although the 18- and 22-foot Sportsman models were left behind, the Sportsman name, so long a badge of quality, value, and practicality for Chris-Craft, soldiered on. The 17-foot Sportsman, described as the "price leader" of the 1955 fleet (ignoring the new value line, the plywood Cavaliers), was styled traditionally and featured a V-windshield. It sold for $2,740 when equipped with the 105-horsepower KL engine, or almost $600 less than an 18-foot Holiday series of that year with the same powerplant.

The 17-foot runabout that was sold as the second-generation Rocket from 1953 to 1954 disappeared from the lineup in 1955, but bounced back in 1956, sharing the 17-foot Sportsman hull and one-piece plastic wrap around windshield that made both boats seem at least from the same family as the Capri. As with the Sportsman, the 17-foot runabout could be had with any one of the K-series engines.

To make your 17 feet of real Chris-Craft-grade mahogany into a Custom cost all of $85, which included a chromium-plated stem band, a cockpit

SHOWBOATS FOR 1956 Chris★Craft
WORLD'S LARGEST BUILDERS OF MOTOR BOATS

In 1956, Chris-Craft returned to the Showboats theme used in 1956, promoting the Constellation and the Capri Runabout on the cover.

paneled with mahogany, and bright finish and linoleum on the floor. The runabout sold modestly—330 units in runabout trim through 1958, whereas the 17-foot Sportsman attracted 1,532 buyers through 1959. By then, the 17-footers were replaced by a utility-style 17-foot Ski Boat, which had similar styling and slightly more beam.

There were other Sportsman models as well. In 1956, when the 25-foot Holiday series was discontinued, a 20-foot Sportsman was included in the catalog. It, too, continued through 1959 but sold modestly compared to the up-and-coming Cavalier line. Among the cruisers, the 29-foot series included an open-hulled boat with a painted hull called a Sportsman.

The Plywood Revolution

Even as the mahogany-planked Chris-Craft lineup evolved, it was clear that in order for the company to grow, it needed to expand beyond the traditional carvel-hulled boats for which Chris-Craft was known. Other builders were making inroads using new fiberglass technology, and fiberglass was a material that the Smiths looked at with skepticism. But Chris-Craft did have experience with plywood—during the war, and through the first half of the 1950s in its Kit Boat Division. Consequently, as the company moved to expand its offerings, plywood would play an integral role.

The Kits were enjoying healthy sales—so much so that it made sense to begin selling some of the Kit models pre-built, such as the 20-foot Gay Paree outboard and a 16-foot Express Cruiser. The Kit Boat fleet also included playful model names such as the 12-foot single-cockpit Meteor and 12-foot utility-style Vagabond; the 14-foot dual cockpit Barracuda with walk-through center deck; the 14-foot Caribbean, Zephyr, and Dolphin; the 15-foot Marlin; the 18-foot Fiesta; and the 21-foot Monterey Express. The big 31-foot Express Cruiser was

dropped, but the mainstay utility and express cruiser models became the foundation of the new Plywood Boat Division, a direct outgrowth of the Kit Boats.

Enter the Cavalier

Knowing which Kit Boats sold best, Chris-Craft selected five pre-built plywood models to offer in 1955. Utilities included a 15-foot Cavalier (60-horsepower inboard, $1,595) and a 17-foot Cavalier (131-horsepower inboard that gave it 40 mile-per-hour speed, $1,795), and the Gay Paree 20-footer, available configured for outboard or inboard power with speeds up to 25 miles per hour, starting at $1,099. Cruisers included a little outboard 16-foot Express two-sleeper that started at $699 and a 21-foot Cabin Cruiser—inboard or twin-outboard—with room for a toilet and with cruiser amenities such as icebox, sink, and stove available as options.

The plywood boats were built primarily in Caruthersville, Missouri, on the Mississippi River, and in Salisbury, Maryland, where the new Sea Skiff line was under full steam. Given that the plywood boats were meant to provide good value for the money, standard equipment was kept to a minimum—lights, bow and stern poles, and windshield. Additional instruments and features such as ammeter, oil pressure gauge, tach-ometer, auto bailer, dock lines, lifting rings, seat cushions, and even the shipping cradle, cost extra.

Among the "Value-packed Chris-Craft Plywood Boats for 1956" as the sales brochure touted, "The Three Cavaliers" included a new 20-footer. Two of these three models proved tremendously popular—the 15-foot Cavalier Utility sold 1,096 units from early 1955 through mid-1959, with another 128 going out the door as Cavalier Runabouts. The 17-footer sold 936 units in utility configuration and 104 in runabout trim during that same period, with its popularity due in part to the fact that it could handle the

Above: Strong performance and even stronger marketing muscle from the world's largest builder of motorboats helped Sea Skiffs develop a reputation for seaworthiness. The 22-footer was the first of the Sea Skiff models introduced by Chris-Craft.

Right: The Sea Skiffs, built in a new plant in Salisbury, Maryland, featured plywood strakes glued with Chris-Craft Sealer, though copper clout nails and brass screws were also used. Decking was made of mahogany plywood. This 1956 22-footer, *Happiness Is*, holds its own among premier vintage mahogany at the Antique Boat Show in Clayton, New York.

Highlights of the Chris-Craft lineup as promoted on the back page of the 1956 catalog. The Constellation model of cruiser had expanded to include various lengths. By this time, the white bow caps that distinguished the cruisers of the early 1950s had disappeared, though the bull-nose was still prevalent.

38-FT. CORSAIR

46-FT. CONSTELLATION

23-FT. EXPRESS CRUISER

38-FT. CONSTELLATION

26-FT. SEMI-ENCLOSED CRUISER

19-FT. CAPRI

23-FT. CONTINENTAL

35-FT. CONSTELLATION

131-horsepower, six-cylinder inboard, which made it a 38 mile-per-hour boat for $2,585. As a double cockpit forward runabout, it cost more than $1,000 less than a comparably powered 19-foot Capri and $500 less than the 17-foot Sportsman. The larger V-20 Utility could also take the bigger engine, but its sales were far less successful, with only forty built over a one-year period. As it had always been at Chris-Craft, less-expensive boats attracted buyers, and unit sales of the Cavaliers compared to those of rivaling traditionally planked boats. So successful were the Cavaliers that in 1957 the Plywood Boat Division became the Cavalier Division.

The plywood cruiser lineup expanded as well in 1956 with the addition of a 22-foot Four-Sleeper Express Cruiser with Flying Bridge that could be configured for one of two inboards or with room for two outboards. The 22-foot Four-Sleeper would sell 406 units through 1958, plus another 303 in Two-Sleeper configuration.

Sea Skiff Success

The gut-wrenching decision to close the petcock on the Outboard Engine Division did have benefits; it allowed Chris-Craft to pour its considerable resources into expanding its real business—building boats. After scanning the pleasure-boating industry for potential growth, the company zeroed in on a traditional craft that was gaining popularity—the lapstrake skiff. Following the methods the Smiths had used before, Chris-Craft started with a close examination of the competition to gain an understanding of not only what characteristics made the boats popular, but also how Chris-Craft could improve them—and build them more cost-effectively, of course.

Two products helped Chris-Craft do just that. Reaching back to its experience building Higgins-spec landing craft in World War II, it developed its new round-bilge lapstrake hulls using strakes made of 3/8-inch marine plywood, held together in part with Thiokol adhesive sealant. In the tradition of Chris-Craft-grade mahogany, the company renamed the Thiokol product "Chris-Craft Sea Skiff Sealer." Decking was mahogany plywood with a traditional mahogany transom.

By 1954 construction was under way in Salisbury, Maryland, of a new factory designed exclusively for the production of the new Sea Skiff line. The first production model was the 22-foot open Sea Skiff, priced at $2,900.

Motor Boating announced the new division of Chris-Craft:

> A new Sea Skiff Division of the Chris-Craft Corporation has been formed to produce a complete line of round bilge, lapstrake boats. The first model, a 22-footer, is already available in dealer showrooms in many parts of the country. Features include a big open cockpit, a private compartment forward, and a choice of either 60 or 95 HP engine. A special synthetic-rubber planking compound is applied to the area of the planks that are to overlap. Planking is drawn up tight with copper clout nails and brass screws.

For the 1955 model year, the Sea Skiff Division launched its assault on Lyman, Century, and other traditional skiff builders by expanding the Sea Skiff lineup substantially. An 18-footer targeted Lyman's Islander and Century's Viking models. Two 26-foot models were offered, an Open and an Enclosed Cruiser Flybridge Four-sleeper. Thirty-footers were also available Open

or as Flybridge or Semi-Enclosed Two- or Four-sleeper Cruisers. A 40-foot cruiser, offered in Flybridge or Semi-Enclosed trim and powered by dual 200-horsepower Chryslers, was added for 1956.

Mid-1950s Cruisers

The effort to freshen the look of the Chris-Craft lineup in 1955 extended to the mahogany cruisers as well as to the sport boats. Add in the acquisition of Roamer, the steel-hulled cruiser company, and the addition of cruisers in the Plywood Boat and Sea Skiff Divisions, and Chris-Craft's overall cruiser offerings were booming.

The 1955 cruiser models abandoned the turtleback bow caps that marked the postwar designs before them. Instead, simple mahogany shear rails met at the stem, as first introduced on the Corsair in 1954, which gave the entire cruiser fleet a new look. As with the sport boats, the cruisers were organized by series, including Express Cruisers of 23, 25, and 27 feet; a 26-foot Series of Sedans and Semi-Enclosed (plus the 27-foot Sedan Flying Bridge model); a new 29-foot Series that included an open Sportsman model; and the Capitan, a 37-foot Series in Commander and Corvette model trim. The 42-foot Series included Express Cruiser, Commander, and Commodore models. The 53-foot Conqueror remained but was joined by another 53-foot model, which in name would continue to the bitter end of the wooden Chris-Craft fleet: the Constellation, described by *Motor Boating* as "a flush deck motor yacht that sleeps 10 in solid sea-going comfort." Fifty-three-foot Connies started coming off the line in Algonac in May of 1954, with forty-two built in the first year. In 1956 the big Constellation was listed as a 54-footer, with another thirty-eight sold, and the Constellation name would extend to 35-, 38-, and 46-footers as well.

New for 1956 among the mahogany cruisers was the 33-foot Futura. Outfitted with a teak

Small cruisers such as *Witness*, a 1956 Semi-Enclosed, met the demands of the burgeoning consumer culture of the 1950s. Chris-Craft offered boaters the opportunity to buy into the boating boom at an affordable level, with dreams of Motor Yachts sending breadwinners back to the office after a relaxing weekend on the water.

cockpit and decks and sporting walk-around decks, the Futura, with its curved clipper stem, foreshadowed a look that would remain with Chris-Craft's wood cruisers through the end of production. The roof extended beyond the forward windshield to form a protective visor, a design element that would also eventually reach the rest of the cruiser lineup. The Futura introduced the use of the corporate double "C" scroll as an extension of the rub rail.

Among the options in 1956 were painted black hull sides. The 42-foot Corsair and the 54-foot Constellation were illustrated in the sales catalog with gleaming black hulls. The interiors of many of the cruiser models continued to use blonde Korina paneling, and cruisers with painted interiors incorporated what we today would consider quintessential 1950s colors: shades of pink, coral, turquoise, and other designer colors.

Above: The gracious interior of the Futura, in all of its 1950s style, included a galley.

Left: Chris-Craft designers signaled a new direction with the introduction of the aptly named 33-foot Futura in 1956, such as *Lizzy*, pictured here. Gone was the bulbous bull-nose in favor of a sleeker clipper-stem bow treatment that other Chris-Craft cruisers would later emulate. It sported walk-around decks, and the roof extended beyond the forward windshield to form a protective visor.

In 1955, in a somewhat serendipitous move, Chris-Craft acquired the Roamer Boat Company of Holland, Michigan, builders of high-quality steel-hulled cruisers. The company was located not far from Chris-Craft's own Holland plant, making takeover logistics convenient. Harry Coll, who had been in charge of the Holland factory, headed up the new Roamer Division. At the time of acquisition, the Roamer Boat Company was building 34-foot express cruisers, 41-foot DCEB cruisers, and 45-foot steel tugs for the Army. The Roamer line would expand to include aluminum hulls and models up to 73 feet.

63

Chris-Craft designers paid unabashed homage to the Detroit auto industry with the 21-foot Continental, which sported tail fins reminiscent of the Chevy Bel Air. *Peggy Sue* is a 1957 21-foot Continental.

Chapter Four

1957–1958
The Super Fleet
Goes Automotive

Chris-Craft was never a company to run out of energy for change, and even after the sweeping redesign of its lineup in 1955, the company continued to look for ways to make certain its boats boosted the adrenaline of prospective customers. An increasing number of fiberglass boat manufacturers were wowing the public with a flotilla of more complex, come-hither shapes and styling than ever before seen in the boating industry. Despite the ultimate sales disappointment of the 1955 Cobra, Chris-Craft design and marketing types believed they had to offer more radical designs to complement, and perhaps lead, their lineup of traditionally planked sport boats.

The Smiths were clever enough to recognize that their dominant position in the powerboat market was anything but secure. With more and more baby-boom boaters entering the market, more and more boat builders were looking to take a piece of that market. Chris-Craft's strengths—its history dating to 1922, its strong, closely held family management, and a seemingly impregnable brand identity—were also weaknesses. The Smiths were trying to run a world-wide manufacturing concern from the relatively small town of Algonac, Michigan, where cold winters not only created difficult conditions for testing and development but also made it tough to recruit the best and the brightest in the marine industry. With more boats ending up in Florida as the Sunshine State built its reputation as a vacation and retirement haven, it made sense to locate a state-of-the-art Manufacturing and Engineering Center at a new world headquarters there.

And so they did. Chris-Craft acquired land in Pompano Beach and relocated from Algonac in late 1957. The move caused no lack of disappointment in Algonac, where many employees felt betrayed. Although there had been bitter labor disputes at times, generations of workers believed they had much to do with making Chris-Craft the world's largest builder of powerboats over the previous 35 years, and in one sudden move, the company was gone. The Algonac facility was not shut down completely at the time, but in retrospect, it was a signal that the end of an era was approaching.

For the Smiths, however, the move to a sunnier climate was a business decision, not unlike any number of other difficult choices they had made over the course of the company's history, decisions that had enabled it to thrive. With the arrival of the late 1950s, Chris-Craft was under pressure to continue its phenomenal growth, to replace its aging six-cylinder Hercules-block engines with V-8 power, and to take more seriously the increasingly popular and successful fiberglass outboards, which

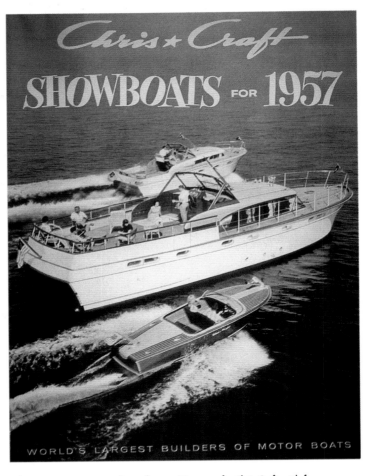

The year 1957 was something of a transition year for Chris-Craft, with fewer new model introductions—though the 38-foot Sport Fisherman did provide Chris-Craft with an entry into a growing niche. The black-and-white catalog cover was dominated by the big Constellation with the Capri Runabout in the foreground.

The 1957 20-foot Continental, such as *Sweet Caroline II*, did not mimic its 21-foot older sister but reflected the look of the Continental as introduced two years earlier.

required different materials and construction techniques than the company's meticulously planned production lines called for. Chris-Craft was also under pressure from the previous generation to begin thinking about cashing out the family business that had made the Smiths wealthy.

It was perhaps for the latter reason that in 1958 Chris-Craft named Harry Coll president. Coll, who had gone to college with Chairman of the Board Harsen Smith and who had worked with Chris-Craft for years, overseeing the Holland plant as well as the Outboard Motor Division, was well equipped to handle the job. He was, however, the first Chris-Craft president in 36 years without the familiar name of Smith.

Going Automotive

For Chris-Craft, 1957 was something of a transition year, with fewer model changes as the company built and settled into new quarters. But it was the first year for a rather striking new design unlike any other in the Chris-Craft fleet to date. Looking to capitalize on the considerable marketing muscle of the car industry, the new 21-foot Continental sported twin tail fins in a look that aped the 1957 Chevrolet Bel Air. Featuring a curved glass windshield, the kingplank was a broad racing stripe in white. The bull-nose bow, crowned with a star, was also white and carried a broad stripe that flowed along the sides and extended to the rear fins, which housed the exhaust vents. The white aft deck drooped down toward the transom, mimicking the trunk of an

Although listed in sales literature as part of the Capri Series of Runabouts, the Silver Arrow was, strictly speaking, a utility-style boat with an open aft area that made this "sports car for the waterways" a bit more practical for water-skiing. Alas, it did not catch on, and only ninety-two were built in two years of production. *Karine N. Rodengen*

Chris-Craft made another bold styling statement in 1958 with the introduction of the 19-foot Silver Arrow. Intended to be a fiberglass design, the Silver Arrow came to market with a traditionally wooden-planked bottom, with fiberglass forming the hull from the chine up, including the distinctive tail fins.

automobile. Among the engine options was the marinized Cadillac V-8, which listed as putting out 300 horsepower and gave the 21-footer a top speed of 43 miles per hour.

The same 21-foot hull was used to create a similarly styled runabout, the 21-foot Capri, which took the place of the previous Riviera-based 21-foot Capri and was introduced for 1958. The double-cockpit Capri's aft deck sloped from the rear of the aft cockpit to the transom and, like the Continental, featured an automotive-style interior. The cockpit was ventilated via a distinctive air scoop on the forward deck, and a sliding fiberglass hardtop was an available option.

However, the overtly automotive styling fared hardly better on the sales floors of Chris-Craft dealerships than the vertical-finned Cobra—only forty-four units of the Continental-based 21-foot Capri were built from 1957 to 1959. The 21-foot Continental sold a little better over the same period, with 190 going out the factory doors.

The postwar bleached mahogany two-tone look had not been banished from the Chris-Craft kingdom. In fact, in 1958, Chris-Craft restyled the 17-foot runabout with the familiar two-tone deck planking. It featured a gentle barrelback stern and shared a pointed bow with the 17-foot Sportsman. As with the shared hulls of the Continental and Capri, the utility configuration of the 17-footers

Before the Silver Arrow was the Lake 'n' Sea fiberglass outboards, the product of a company purchased by Chris-Craft in 1957. Delamination problems shook the Smiths' confidence, and they sold Lake 'n' Sea shortly after acquiring it. This is a 1959 model.

proved far more popular than the runabout—more than 1,000 17-foot Sportsman were built between 1956 and 1959, compared with 236 of the 17-foot runabout. In 1959 the runabout was replaced by a utility-style 17-foot Ski Boat,

The 1958 18-foot Continental was a solidly successful model. First introduced for 1955, the 18-footers were built through 1960, selling nearly 1,000 units overall. *Karine N. Rodengen*

which had very similar styling and slightly more beam.

Chris-Craft and Fiberglass

Another remarkable styling highlight of the late 1950s was the radically designed Silver Arrow, which was launched in 1958 as Chris-Craft's first fiberglass boat and was called by the company the "sports car of the waterways." Although by 1955 boat manufacturers had built an estimated 40,000 fiberglass boats—most of them small

outboards—Chris-Craft had been slow to embrace production of these boats, but that is not to say that the company had not been experimenting. Elements of cruiser cabins were made of fiberglass, and the 1955 Cobra cowling and the large dorsal fin were fiberglass. In 1957, Chris-Craft purchased a small maker of fiberglass runabouts, Lake 'n' Sea, but delamination problems led to a poor reputation, and the Smiths soon sold the company.

While development of fiberglass was proceeding at a fast and furious pace in the pleasure-boat

This 1958 19-foot Capri was in many ways a quintessential Chris-Craft for its day. Featuring styling reminiscent of predecessors such as the 20-foot Custom and Riviera, it also included 1950s elements such as the wraparound windshield. *Karine N. Rodengen*

industry (the largest manufacturer, Glasspar, had five factories that churned out a total of 16,000 boats in 1959), there were still doubts about the material's durability—especially in the executive suite at Chris-Craft. So when the 19-foot Silver Arrow was finally unveiled, listed in the 1958 sales literature as part of the Capri Series of Runabouts, it sported a conventional wood-bottomed hull that used fiberglass to create flowing lines from the chine up, including wing-like tail fins that extended from the sides at the stern. With Century and Correct Craft garnering reputations for superior ski boats, the Silver Arrow was advertised by Chris-Craft as a "sports car for the waterways" that was a "honey for water skiing."

Strictly speaking, the Silver Arrow was a utility-style hull, with an open aft area and engine cover rather than enclosed cockpit, which made it far more practical than, for example, the single-cockpit Cobra. Unfortunately, its half-wood and half-fiberglass construction made for a boat that

weighed more than 2,770 pounds, a whopping 400 pounds heavier than the 18-foot Continental or Capri.

Chris-Craft gave the Silver Arrow more of a chance in the market than it gave the Cobra—not only did it remain in the lineup for two model years, but the appearance of the Silver Arrow in the 1958 lineup was at least part of the reason the Riviera-style Capris were shelved, along with the production of the 20-foot Holiday and Continental models. Clearly, the Silver Arrow was meant to win over the sport boat public.

Alas, it did not, as only ninety-two units were manufactured. It did not help, perhaps, that when equipped with the new Chevy-based Chris-Craft 283 V-8 engine, the Silver Arrow listed for the high price of $6,200 in 1958. The price was cut more than $1,000 in 1959, but a comparably powered 18-foot Continental, also a 40-mile-per-hour boat, could be had for $4,270.

Plywood Comes of Age

While Chris-Craft management was disappointed and frustrated with the sales results of its early attempts at incorporating fiberglass into its mainstream fleet, the new value line was going gangbusters. The Plywood Boat Division, which came into existence in 1955 as a natural outgrowth of the Kit Boats, was renamed once again in 1957, becoming the Cavalier Division after the model name of the early pre-built plywood utilities. Having abandoned the Lake 'n' Sea small fiberglass outboard

The Sea Skiff line continued to expand in 1958, including fifteen different models in seven different hull lengths from 18 to 40 feet. *Razz Matazz* is a 26-foot Open Sea Skiff. The 26-foot hull was available in other configurations as well, including a Fisherman with a fishing bridge.

experiment, Chris-Craft concentrated on positioning its Cavalier plywood boats as legitimate competition for the other upstart fiberglass boat companies.

In addition, the Kit Boats, sporting trendy design cues and available at bargain prices for the do-it-yourself crowd, continued to find buyers. This was due in part to the continued improvement and reliability of available outboard power.

Although Chris-Craft had given up on its own outboard division in 1953 (leaving behind designs for a 25-horsepower two-stroke and four-stroke V-4), other manufacturers such as Mercury and Johnson had successfully brought to market lighter, more powerful engines that sold enough units to be cost-effective. Chris-Craft was determined to supply the boats for those outboard engines.

From *Chris ★ Craft*
World's greatest values in low-cost boating!

Cavalier Boats
DIVISION OF CHRIS ★ CRAFT CORPORATION

REGISTERED U.S. PATENT OFFICE

NEW 1958 CAVALIER BOATS

17-ft. Cavalier Utility (left); 19-ft. Semi-Enclosed Outboard Sports Cruiser

The 1958 Kit Boat catalog promoted the 17-foot Cavalier Utility and 19-foot Semi-Enclosed Sports Cruiser, which were also available prebuilt from the newly named Cavalier Division (neé Plywood Boat Division).

75

By the time *Onaway*, this 1957 24-foot Chris-Craft cruiser, hit the water, its distinctive bull-nose bow was on its way out in favor of the clipper stem seen first on the Futura and then on the Sport Fisherman. Pocket cruisers from the plywood Cavalier line also proved popular among value-oriented boaters.

Kit Boat models were revamped in 1957, and the 14-foot Grayling and 15-foot Tarpon were added. In some cases, the Kit lineup mimicked the mainstream lineup, such as with the 12-foot Meteor and 14-foot Comet Kits, which sprouted tail fins like the 21-foot Continental and the 21-foot Capri of similar vintage in the standard Chris-Craft lineup. A fleet of Kit 19-footers, including a Sports Express Cruiser, Sports Runabout, and Sports Convertible—all utility-style boats that could be built

Chris✦Craft 65-FT. CONSTELLATION

Chris✦Craft 65-FT. MOTOR YACHT

Topping the cruiser line was one of the longest standard hull lengths in Chris-Craft's history, a 65-foot hull available either as the Motor Yacht or in Constellation trim, as featured in the 1958 catalog.

either as outboards or inboards—mirrored the pre-built Cavalier Express and Cavalier Semi-Enclosed 19-footers in the Cavalier Division. Likewise, the new 22-foot Express Cruiser, available as a Kit, was simultaneously enjoying considerable popularity as a pre-built Cavalier.

When Chris-Craft started marketing the pre-built plywood boats in 1955, it began with five models, and in 1956 the company added the 20-foot V-20 Utility and 22-foot Two- and Four-Sleeper.

In 1957 the 21-foot Cabin Cruiser would lose favor (after selling nearly 300 units) to a newcomer, the 19-foot Cavalier Express, which sold for $3,350 when powered by a 95-horsepower K engine that gave it 30 miles per hour. A year later, the boat was also offered as the VS-19 Cavalier Semi-Enclosed. Combined sales for the 19-footers were 272 units through 1959. A revamped outboard 16-foot Cavalier Semi-Enclosed Sports Cruiser was introduced in 1957 as well and sold for $1,025, plus $19 for the cradle and $10 to load the boat onto the cradle. The same hull was also available as a Sports Utility, though far fewer of those were sold.

By 1958 it was clear that the Cavalier line was the future for Chris-Craft's plywood boats, and the company began selling the Kits at bargain prices to get rid of inventory. That would continue into 1959, when the Cavalier line came into its own.

The Skiffs Fill Out

Having successfully launched its copycat Sea Skiffs—lapstrake skiffs built with plywood strakes, Sea Skiff Sealer (Thiokol), and copper clout nails—in 1954, Chris-Craft looked to expand the Sea Skiff lineup as it had in the Cavalier lineup. In 1957 the company offered an enclosed fly bridge on the 26-foot Sea Skiff and offered the 30-footer as an Open model as well as Semi-Enclosed.

For the 1958 model year, as with the traditional lineups, there were more changes, which led to fifteen different models in seven different hull lengths. New was the 22-foot Ranger that offered V-berths under a beamy foredeck and provided modest overnight accommodations. The Ranger could be had in either a Two-Sleeper or Trunk Cabin model. The boats grew larger, with a 40-foot hull available as a semi-enclosed cruiser or convertible sedan. To satisfy sport fishermen who preferred the reputation for stability that a lapstrake skiff offered, the 30-, 35-, and 40-foot models were all available with a fishing bridge, and the 26-footer could be had as the Fisherman model as well.

Although Chris-Craft was making headway with its Sea Skiff line, competition was still significant, as Lyman, Century, and traditional skiff builders battled for their share of the market. Chris-Craft looked to solidify a hold on the skiff market by trumpeting the strength and reliability

of their skiff-building methods and offering extras like five additional hull colors in addition to the traditional white. Chris-Craft may have been late to the lapstrake regatta, but it brought its marketing muscle and will to win.

Cruisers Grow Up

While Chris-Craft sport boats may have been better known to the average American boater in the 1950s, Chris-Craft's cruiser fleet continued to expand. The Constellation, offered in 35-, 38-, 42-, 46-, and 55-foot lengths, dominated a lineup in 1957 that also included the popular 23-foot Express Cruiser, 32-foot Commander, 33-foot Futura Express, 38- and 42-foot Corsair, 55-foot Conqueror, and 56-foot Salon Motor Yacht. A new 38-foot Sport Fisherman, which featured the clipper stem styling used on the 33-foot Futura Express in 1956, was introduced for 1957.

In 1958, Chris-Craft reached back some 30 years in reviving the Cadet and Commuter model names. The Cadet name, originally Chris-Craft's second runabout model introduced in 1927, adorned a 25-foot fly bridge Sedan in the cruiser lineup. The Commuter, known today as the name of Chris-Craft's first stock cruiser, a 38-footer introduced in 1929, was in 1958 the moniker adorning a fast (36 miles per hour with twin 175-horsepower engines) new 26-footer that shared a hull with a 26-foot Sports Express.

Chris-Craft also expanded the upper echelon of its stock cruiser fleet in 1958, adding a 65-foot hull that could be purchased as a Constellation or Motor Yacht, the latter selling for more than $160,000. These two models represented Chris-Craft's largest standard hull lengths, outgrowing the 1950 62-foot Motor Yacht by 3 feet.

Assuming that those who could afford such a boat could and would also afford to hire a captain to pilot her, the elite Motor Yacht featured a pilot house, captain's cabin, and crew's quarters. A wide

Chris-Craft made a somewhat serendipitous purchase of Roamer, builder of steel-hulled cruisers, in 1955. Roamer was located in Holland, Michigan, not far from Chris-Craft's own plant, where many of its mahogany cruisers were built. Shown here is the 1958 Roamer Riviera 42, a model that revived the model name of Chris-Craft's early 1950s runabout.

forward deck was open to the sun, and a canopied aft deck provided cover and comfort for owners and their guests. The galley was supplemented with a separate dining salon, the owner's stateroom, and two guest staterooms.

It was a far cry from the cramped quarters of an outboard express cruiser, as well as testament to the notion that Chris-Craft owned the leisure-craft waters, from the top of the market down. It would be hard to believe the company would introduce the industry's first all-fiberglass cruiser just six years later, or that the last wood cruiser, a Constellation, would come out of the Holland plant in less than 15 years.

In order to compete with builders like Correct Craft and Century, whose models had developed a good reputation among water sports fans in the 1950s, Chris-Craft introduced the 17-foot Ski Boat in 1959. The utility-style Ski Boat, such as *Summer of '59*, was powered by the all-new Chris-Craft 283 V-8, which made it a 40-mile-per-hour boat. *Karine N. Rodengen*

Chapter Five

1959–1960

Birth of the Ski Boat, Death of the Runabout

From the outside looking in, 1959 represented the peak of Chris-Craft's influence, the result of decades of building powerboats with an unparalleled combination of quality, efficiency, and innovation. The modest family business that started in 1922 with an idea for producing standardized runabouts fitted out with World War I surplus airplane engines had grown to become, as the Smiths routinely claimed, the world's largest builder of motorboats.

That image was bolstered still further in May 1959 when, as boaters and would-be boaters in northern climes were preparing for another summer season on the water, the cover of *Time* magazine announced "The New Boom in Boating." The article, in part, said, "The sport that 20 years ago was confined largely to fishermen and the rich has become a pastime enjoyed by some 40 million U.S.

citizens. In just twelve years the number of boats that churn the U.S.'s waterways has more than tripled, has more than tripled, from 2,5000,000 to nearly 8,000,000. And the boom is still growing."

And who was the leader of this boom? None other than Harsen Alfred Smith, the third-generation head of Chris-Craft, whose mildly amused mug appeared on the cover of the *Time* boating boom issue as the man in charge of a $40 million outfit putting out 8,000 boats annually from nine U.S. factories. The article was a virtual love letter about the Smiths and their highly successful boat-building venture.

But looking out from inside the boardroom at Chris-Craft, the horizon was a bit cloudier. Or,

perhaps, all too clear. The day of the traditional runabout seemed to be over, as sales of Capris, the last of the cockpitted models in the Chris-Craft lineup, had dwindled to mere dozens annually. Although Harsen was quoted as saying that he did not consider outboards a threat to inboards, five million Americans were happily boating with reliable and powerful outboard motors strapped to their transoms, and many of those boats were made from fiberglass. While by 1959 Chris-Craft had build boats of metal (Roamer) and had created the half-glass Silver Arrow, Harsen had confessed to *Time* that the company's heart was with wood. It would take energy, capital, and, above all, desire to keep the

Luxury cruising, fishing, and water-skiing were the focus of the models featured on Chris-Craft's 1959 catalog cover. Both the Silver Arrow and 17-foot Ski Boat were promoted as superior for water-skiing, the Sport Fisherman looked to cash in on the latest craze among big-game anglers, and the luxury yachts were meant to compete among yacht builders such as Trumphy, Burger, and Grebe.

The venerable six-cylinder 95-horsepower K engine was the backbone of the Hercules-block Chris-Craft marine-engine fleet for more than 20 years, and many continue to provide reliable service today. This K still powers a 1956 22-foot Sea Skiff.

world's largest builder of motorboats at the head of the fleet in the coming decade.

All New Power

Among the improvements that Chris-Craft had been hard at work on was finding replacements for the aging Model A and Model B engines, as well as the K-series, M-series, and W-series straight four- and six-cylinder engines that had been powering its boats for 25 years. Throughout the 1950s, the engine division had been eking more power out of their Hercules-based marine

inboards—engines that were first developed two decades before.

As the economy had emerged from the Depression in the 1930s, Chris-Craft needed a plentiful and affordable supply of engines to replace the big V-8 A-70 and A-120 engines Jay W. Smith had developed in the late 1920s and to supplement the Chrysler fours. The solution was a line of engines based on a Hercules block and built for marine use by Chris-Craft. First came the Model A and Model B four-cylinder engines, which generated around 55 horsepower and were

Chris Craft

V8 POWER
...yours in every
CAVALIER

World's greatest value in marine engines — more horsepower per pound than any other V8! Famous for smooth performance, rugged dependability, compact design, operating economy!

Top to bottom, 30-ft. Cavalier Express Cruiser, 25-ft. Cavalier Express Cruiser, 18-ft. Cavalier Sports Utility.

CAVALIER DIVISION, CHRIS-CRAFT CORPORATION, POMPANO BEACH, FLORIDA
World's Largest Builders of Motor Boats

Model "283" V8
develops 185-hp

NOTES PERTAINING TO ALL MODELS
All speeds shown herein attained over certified course, under favorable conditions, or are estimated and not guaranteed. Prices and specifications contained in this literature are based on the latest product information available at the time of publication approval. The right is reserved to make changes at any time without notice in prices, colors, materials, equipment, specifications, and models, and also to discontinue models. Approved accessories for factory installation shown, and special equipment such as dishes, curtains, compasses, special electrical equipment, radios, etc., pictured but not listed as standard equipment or approved accessories, will be furnished on request at extra cost, if available.

copyright 1960 Chris-Craft Corp.   Litho in U.S.A.

By 1960, Chris-Craft had established the new 283 V-8 as its engine of choice, not only in the traditional mahogany boats but in the value-oriented Cavaliers as well. Based on the Chevy small block and marinized by Chris-Craft, the 283 made 185 horsepower.

earmarked for use in smaller runabouts and utilities and small cruisers. The Model B was tweaked in 1954 to up it to 60 horsepower, and reintroduced in two versions, the basic Model A and the Model B, which had more transmission options. The Model A and Model B continued to be used into the 1960s and even provided power for the 35-foot Motor Sailer.

The real heart of the Chris-Craft engine family, however, was the six-cylinder K series. The K was based on a Hercules straight-six L-head industrial engine block that had proven itself rugged and reliable when used as a truck engine or with irrigation pumps that needed to run continuously while providing a reasonable horsepower-to-weight ratio. Marine engine manufacturers such as Kermath and Scripps also used Hercules blocks. Chris-Craft manufactured an estimated 200,000 units of the K series, many of which were sold to other boat builders.

The first K engine, 221.4 ci that generated 85 horsepower at 3,300 rpm, was introduced in the

The 1959 24-foot Sportsman featured a clipper bow, mahogany-framed windshield, and enough space under the forward deck for a head.

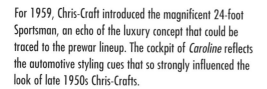

For 1959, Chris-Craft introduced the magnificent 24-foot Sportsman, an echo of the luxury concept that could be traced to the prewar lineup. The cockpit of *Caroline* reflects the automotive styling cues that so strongly influenced the look of late 1950s Chris-Crafts.

1937 lineup. Two years later it was bored out to 229.7 ci, which gave it 95 horsepower. The 95-horsepower K was a stalwart of the Chris-Craft line for years, powering generations of Chris-Crafts. In 1959 the same basic engine went to 100 horsepower. It was finally discontinued in 1963.

For those in search of more power, the KB model featured triple Zenith downdraft carbs, a lighter flywheel, and a high-performance cam, and generated a total of 121 horsepower at 3,800 rpm. Then in 1948, Chris-Craft came out with the most powerful of the K-series engines, the 131-hp KBL, a longstroke version of the KB that increased displacement to 236.6 ci by increasing the stroke. The KBL was replaced by the KFL after 1956, swapping the triple downdraft carbs for dual updraft models, with no reduction in horsepower. The KFL survived into 1960.

In 1949 the standard KL longstroke version of the K was introduced using the standard flywheel and single carb and generating 105 horsepower. In 1951, Chris-Craft introduced the KLC, a hot-rod version of the longstroke that featured a high-performance cam, lighter flywheel, and higher compression, yielding 120 horsepower. Like the KBL, the KLC remained an option through 1956.

Chris-Craft also used a Hercules-based straight six for its larger 320.4 ci M-series engine, first produced in the late 1930s and generating 130 horsepower. The high-performance MB put out 145 horsepower. After World War II, the ML, or longstroke edition of the M, produced 145 horsepower from an increased 330.2 ci displacement. The longstroke was also hopped up to create the MBL in 1948, putting out 158 horsepower at 3,400 rpm and pushing the postwar 19-foot Racing Runabout, for example, to 44 miles per hour. Even more powerful was the MCL race engine introduced in the 1950s, sucking air through twin updraft carbs on the same longstroke block to make 175 horsepower.

For cruisers, Chris-Craft had a bigger engine yet, the 160-horsepower, 404.3 ci (and weighing more than 1,200 pounds) W series that *Motor Boating* promoted in 1954 as "designed to withstand the rigors of long, continuous service where steady performance and economy of operation are all-important." In 1955, Chris-Craft boosted the W to 190 horsepower and called it the WB, soon after claiming an additional 10 ponies for 200 horsepower at 3,200 rpm.

By the late 1950s, however, all these engines—A&B fours, the K-series, M-series, and W-series—seemed outdated as automakers began to focus on the benefits of V-8 power. In order to compete, Chris-Craft needed a new powerplant.

Chris-Craft's First Modern V-8s

The first of the contemporary V-8s to get stuffed into a Chris-Craft was the Chrysler Hemi. Marinized by Chrysler in the mid-1950s, the result came just in time to find its way under the fiberglass aft cowling of the 21-foot Chris-Craft Cobra for 1955.

The Hemi was a 331 ci overhead valve V-8 that generated 200 horsepower at 4,400 rpm in an 1,100-pound package with downdraft carbs and a six-volt electrical system. The first twenty-one 21-footers were shipped with the Hemis, which gave them 50-plus miles-per-hour top speed.

Another seventeen of the 21-foot Cobras were equipped with a marinized Cadillac overhead valve V-8, an engine that pushed Century Coronados to nearly 60 miles per hour. The engine was developed by Detroit Cadillac dealer Cal Connell, who founded Detroit Racing Equipment (DRE). DRE's 331 ci conversion generated 285 horsepower at 5,200 rpm, thanks to dual four-barrel Rochester carbs. The end result was a top speed of 55 miles per hour for the Cobra.

sporty,
speedy,
quality-built

new 1960
Chris ★ Craft
SPORTS BOATS

By the end of the decade, the fastest and flashiest models in the sport boat category were utility-style boats rather than runabouts. The 1960 sportboat flyer featured the 21-foot Continental.

Chris-Craft continued to offer the Cadillac V-8, upgraded to 365 ci in 1956 and 390 ci in 1959, until the introduction of the marinized version of the Chevy small block. Meanwhile, Connell adopted the name Cadillac Crusader Marine after a 53-foot Constellation that was powered by three of Connell's Cadillacs, leading to the origin Crusader Marine. When Chevrolet introduced its 409 ci engine in the early 60s, Crusader Marine ceased marinizing the Cadillac V-8s and switched to the Chevys.

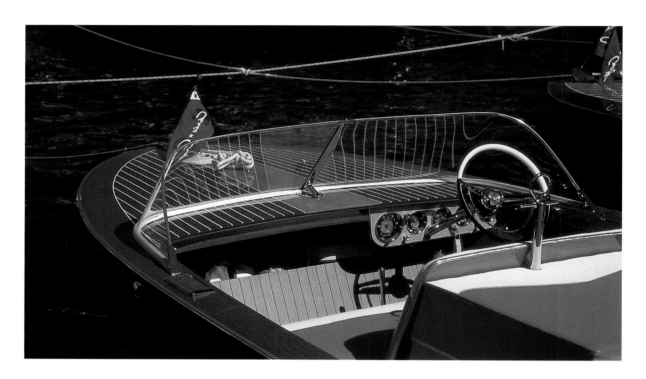

All Hail the Small Block

Marinizing the small-block Chevy for pro-spective boat owners was not only a practical move, since it was a good engine that would be manufactured in huge quantities, driving costs down. It would likely generate showroom interest as well, given that Chris-Craft marketing types had long looked for chances to piggyback on the trends and advertising of car manufacturers. After all, since 1953, Chris-Craft had been using the Chris-O-Matic transmission that featured electric-hydraulic clutch control, which followed the trend of easy-to-use automatic trannys started in the car world.

Chris-Craft introduced its marinized version of the Chevy small-block 283 ci V-8 in 1959. The 185-horsepower 283, which has become a hugely popular engine to modify, was used with great success in Chris-Craft's smaller sport boats on into the 1960s and offered boats like the 17-foot Ski Boat a top speed of 40 miles per hour. It was so well matched to the 17-footer that in 1968 it was incorporated into the model name of the boat: the SS 283 Ski Boat. It was also one of the two choices, along with the venerable K, in the Capri Runabouts that were the last of their line from 1959 to 1961. Twin 283s were common throughout the cruiser lineup as well, and by 1963, the K-series of inline sixes was discontinued.

The 283 wasn't the only V-8 in the lineup, as motorheads' lust for power reached the boat industry during the musclecar era. The 1960s saw the all-American V-8 take charge, as bigger and bigger engines were packed into the utility-style sport boats. The 327F, or Corvette engine, was used in 17- and 18-foot Super Sports and then in the 17- and 20-foot Grand Prix. Chris-Craft also marinized the Ford MEL (Mercury/Edsel/Lincoln) 430 and 431 engines for use in powerboats such as the early-1960s 24-foot Sportsman, 21-foot Continental, and 20-foot Holiday, and to serve as a workhorse in cruisers. In 1966 the Ford 427 got the Chris-Craft marine treatment, powering the 20- and 21-foot Super Sports and later the 20-foot Grand Prix.

Last of the Smith-Built Boats

The 1959 lineup of mahogany Chris-Crafts included a new model, the 17-foot Ski Boat, which was to compete with firms such as Century and Correct Craft, both of which were carving out a reputation as having good boats for the increasingly popular water sports. Fitted with the new 283 engine, the Ski Boat was another 40-mile-per-hour Chris-Craft, following a tradition that reached back to the original 26-foot runabout in the 1920s.

Elsewhere in the sport boat lineup, the popular 18-foot Holiday gave way to the even more popular 18-foot Continental. The 23-foot Continental was also discontinued to make way for a magnificent new 24-foot Sportsman. With a smart clipper bow, mahogany-framed windshield, and enough space under the forward deck for a head, the big Sportsman was another throwback to the prewar days of the luxurious big Sportsman models, only reinvented with automotive styling cues for 1959. Still leading the utility fleet was the big 26-foot Continental that had been in the lineup since 1956.

For other models, 1959 was a closing year. The Silver Arrow never got on plane with the public, although it was offered with the new 283

Introduced in 1959, the 17-foot Ski Boat continued in the Chris-Craft lineup, with modifications, through 1968. It was a steady-selling model, with more than 1,800 units built, and it spawned a plywood version in the Cavalier line starting in 1962. *Infatuation* (top) and *Miss Ski Tow* are both 1959 17-foot Ski Boats.

The Capri Runabout, first introduced in 1955 as a replacement for the Riviera, was reaching the end of its reign when this version was promoted in the 1960 catalog. The last true wooden runabout model made by Chris-Craft, it was discontinued after 1961 by the company's new owners.

V-8 as part of the Capri Series and was touted as good for water skiing. The finned 21-foot Continental and 21-foot Capri also struggled through their final year.

A smaller 18-foot Capri runabout based on the same hull as the 18-foot Continental utility eschewed the flashy tail fins of its bigger sister in favor of the now familiar 1950s look of a blonde mahogany forward kingplank and aft engine hatch cover. In concert with the chrome triangle on the aft sides of the Ski Boat,

the little Capri sported painted white triangles. Only sixty-five were built, but the little Capri would be revamped again the following year, stretched just enough to call it a 19-footer. All of 119 were built, but it would survive into 1961, with the painted triangle giving way to a painted white side panel matching that of the 1961 Continentals. After making sixty more in 1961, the Capri—last of the true wooden Chris-Craft runabouts—was dropped. An era had ended.

This 1961 Continental still used the bleached mahogany highlights on the kingplank, but 1950s style was giving way to the more colorful vinyl look of the 1960s. The inline six Hercules-based engines bowed in deference to the muscle-era power of a marinized Lincoln V-8 that generated 275 horsepower and gave the 21-foot Continental a claimed top speed of 42 miles per hour.

For boat sellers, though, it was of no concern. The open-hulled utilities—popularized first in the 1930s during the Depression—won out as more useful, and were just as fast and sporty as the cockpitted runabouts. Chris-Craft would go on, but the day of the wooden runabout was done.

The Value Line

Part of the reason for the declining sales power of the runabouts, perhaps, was the increasing popularity of Chris-Craft's value-oriented Cavalier line of plywood boats. New in the Cavalier lineup for 1959 was an 18-foot Sports Utility, which joined the 15- and 17-foot hulls as the three utility-style

Right and opposite: In spite of new lapstrake competition from Owens Yacht Company, Chris-Craft continued to expand its Sea Skiff line. This 1959 catalog page features two of the popular larger models in the Sea Skiff fleet: the 30-foot Open with a semi-enclosed top and a 40-foot Semi-Enclosed with the optional fishing bridge.

boats in the Cavalier fleet. Both the 17- and 18-footers could be purchased with the new 185 horsepower V-8, making them 40-mile-per-hour boats at the bargain prices of $2,770 and $2,885, respectively. Most of the 18-footers were sold as the Custom V-8 Sports Utility, which included a glassed bottom, instrumentation, seat cushions, with vinyl flooring as standard, and sold for $3,025. While it was a glassed-over plywood boat, it was nominally still a Chris-Craft.

In 1961 a 19-foot Capri Runabout powered by the 283 V-8 sold for more than $4,200 while offering lower top speed than the 18-foot Cavalier Sports Utility. No surprise, then, that the Cavalier sold over 500 more units than the Capri from 1959 to1961.

Meanwhile, Chris-Craft also used its Sportsman moniker to good effect in the Cavalier lineup. The Kit Boat Division had sold a 21-foot hull as a Sportsman that also could be made as an Express Cruiser. Cavalier continued that strategy in 1960 with a 23-foot Sportsman that was based on the 23-foot Express Cruiser hull, and followed

Round-bilge Lapstrake Boating at its Best

NEW CHRIS-CRAFT SEA SKIFFS

FAST! • DRY! • SEAWORTHY!

Top—40-ft. Semi-Enclosed Cruiser with Fishing Bridge. Center—22-ft. Ranger, 2-Sleeper. Bottom—35-ft. Semi-Enclosed Cruiser.

WORLD'S LARGEST BUILDERS OF SEA SKIFFS

this in 1961 with a 21-foot Sportsman based on the 21-foot Express Cruiser. Equipped with the 185-horsepower V-8, these were fast enough for water skiing and big enough to haul a boatload of baby boomers.

Bargains were also to be had in plywood in cruiser trim. The Cavalier lineup was revamped during 1959, dropping the 16-, 19-, and 22-foot

pocket cruisers to launch a whole new fleet of Express Cruisers, which promised "luxury boating with complete family cruising accommodations at a sensational new low price," with the 23-foot Two-Sleeper, 25-foot Four-Sleeper, and 30-foot Six-Sleeper. Featuring the "New V-8 Power," the 23-footer claimed 35 miles per hour and sold for $4,380; the 25-footer, 33 miles per hour for $5,245; and the 30-footer, 26 miles per hour for $7,880. The 30-foot Express could also be equipped with twin V-8s and gain another 10 miles per hour for $9,695. Standard equipment on the Express Cruisers included a galley with stainless-steel sink and two-burner alcohol stove, vinyl-covered cushions in the berths, a toilet, and instruments. Options included a companion seat, curtains, pilot seat, stern pole and ensign, and a windshield wiper. The 30-footer was described in Chris-Craft literature as having "a long, sleek silhouette. A gracefully

tapering style-line extends full length of the hull, terminating in a bold, stainless steel band—creating a look of motion."

Planked Cruisers

The bull-nose bows that had become such a recognizable characteristic of Chris-Craft's fleet beginning with the Conqueror in 1950 made their final appearance in 1959, another signal that it was not just the end of a decade but the end of an era. The 33-foot Futura Express that launched the clipper stem enjoyed its final year in 1959 as well, though its hull could be seen in the 33-foot Sport Fisherman and 33-foot Sports Cruiser. Overall, the cruiser lineup was trimmed to sixteen models in twelve lengths. Eight of those were Constellations, a name that would eventually ride out the slow decline of the mahogany cruiser over the ensuing decade.

By 1960 the cruiser lineup was dominated by the Constellation model, which made up about half of the available cruisers in a variety of lengths. Shown is the interior of the 28-foot Connie, *Ginny Lou*.

By February 1960, a scant nine months after Harsen Smith graced the cover of *Time* magazine as the chairman of the Smith boat-building empire, the family sold Chris-Craft to National Automotive Fibers, Inc. (NAFI) for a reported $40 million. At the time it was a shock, especially to some of the fifty-five Smith-family stockholders who only heard about the sale after the fact. A *Business Week* article a few months later told a tale of a chance meeting between Owen Smith and NAFI owners at the New York Boat Show in January that led to the sale a month later.

But this was likely just more aw-shucks legend that diverted attention away from one more shrewd business decision—hard though it must have been—by the Smiths. The boat industry was at the end of the wooden boat era, and the Smiths were wooden-boat men. Certainly they would have been capable overseers of the changes that were necessary to convert the company to fiberglass, but perhaps the truth was that they simply weren't interested.

Chris-Craft, under NAFI, continued to build wooden sport boats and cruisers throughout the 1960s, with the last wooden boat, a Constellation, coming off the Holland line in 1972. Many of those models are classics today. But the glory days of the 1950s went out the door in the early 1960s with the departure of the Smiths.

Index

Other MBI Publishing Company titles of interest:

Chris-Craft
ISBN 0-7603-0606-0

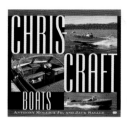

Chris-Craft 1922-1972
ISBN 0-7603-0920-5

Hackercraft
ISBN 0-7603-1107-2

**Classic American Runabouts:
Wood Boats 1915-1965**
ISBN 0-7603-0375-4

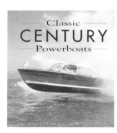

Classic Century Powerboats
ISBN 0-7603-1080-7

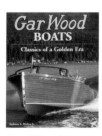

**Gar Wood Boats:
Classics of a Golden Era**
ISBN 0-7603-0607-9

**A Century of Outboard Racing
131986**
ISBN 0-7603-0375-4

**Classic Speedboats 1916-1939
125483**
ISBN 0-7603-0464-5

**Classic Speedboats 1945-1962
130387**
ISBN 0-7603-0916-7

Find us on the internet at www.motorbooks.com 1-800-826-6600